This book is for all of us who were told that we weren't creative enough, talented enough, or skilled enough to accomplish our dreams. You are more than capable. **"…With man this is impossible, but with God all things are possible."**

Acknowledgements

I want to thank God for giving me the vision to write a book and then more importantly surrounding me with excellent people that would help make this dream a reality.

Robert Coats Sr.: Dad, you have been my absolute best friend and mentor since I was born. You are the epitome of what a God Fearing man is and everything that people see is a result of me learning it first from you. Thank you for always being there when I needed you and always staying on me to finish this. Without you this would still not have been completed.

Geraldine Coats: Mom, you have been my inspiration for everything that I have done. Your belief in me at an early age taught me that I could be anything that I ever dreamed of. I thank you for sacrificing your dreams so that your 5 children could have their own. I am forever indebted to you and will retire you soon. Love you.

Andressa, Ayanna, Tamika, and Ryan Coats: My siblings, I could not have picked a better family then you all… I'm lying I can't stand any of you all still! LOL You all are strictly on here because I would have got in trouble with Mom if I didn't make a section for you. I'm not worried because I know none of you all will even read this book past this page. Love you still!

Jerrian Bell: The Best graphic designer in the world. It's because of you that anybody is even holding this book in their hands. I truly appreciate you. You were there through everything and I can't thank you enough for believing in this project! I look forward to nothing but great things from you in life.

Darrell Hunter: The person who makes my writing readable! It took me going through several dozen people to find someone who truly got it! This book would have made no sense if I didn't have you edit it four hundred thousand times. Thank you for your sleepless nights in making this book come to life.

Matthew S. Orr, Trevion Blanding, Shanel Cooper-Sykes, Shaun Derik, Shannon Curtain and Terrence Perkins I thank you all for being there for me through life. Some of you for a longer period then others but you all have made a significant impact on my life. Thank you for your friendship.

Tasha Curtis what can I say about you. You always reminded me through this process to be patient and focus on changing lives instead of just book sales. I thank you for being there for me when I had nothing, I mean absolutely nothing. I thank you especially for always speaking to the King in me instead of the coward. Thank you for simply being you. Your friendship is priceless.

Rachel Young, Tia Coats, Danielle Terreri, Kimberly White and Lynne Williams Editors and Technical Researchers! I thank all of you for your input and time in this project. I spent countless hours on the phone with each and every one of you all and you were so patient with me. I would get one idea from one of you and then run to the next not figuring out until later that you all were so different from the next. It's crazy to work with this many people but this book would not be where it is if it wasn't for you all. You all are amazing and I'm grateful to know each and every one of you.

Pamela Lowery – I thank you for planting the seed in my head that I could do this! If it hadn't been for you telling me this was easy (which it wasn't) I would have never gotten started. Thank you for your belief in me.

Stan Brooks- I thank you for designing all my sites so that people could go on it and purchase this book. You make me look halfway decent on the internet! LOL! But I truly once

again appreciate you for helping build my virtual brand.

Honorable Mention

Carl Mckinney	Addis & Tasha Asmelash
Mark Wolfe	My God Children – Zipporah Asmelash, Michael and Taylor Norman,
James Han	
Elijah Young	Tyree and Tyson Perkins
Travis Fitzwater	George Fraser
Maurice Hall	Ephren Taylor
Makia Kambon	Dezmon Landers
Marina King	Speak Williams
Nate & J'hanna Appleby	Javier Sanchez
Tavyon Green	Eric Troy
Tyler Coles	Phil & Susan Sorentino
Jorianna Revels	Daniel Desta
Kennedy Woods	Jesse Toy
Megan Woods	Isaac Carr
Josh Revels	Ronnie & Elyse Hill

Jay Thomas	Ashlie Jenkins
Brandon Harris	Tye Fletcher
Aunt Renee Coats-Barbour	Jamie Paige
Aunt Mary Coats	Josh Ross
Ian Hall	Jordian Ross
Eric Hall	Donnell Hughes
Shavonne Harris	Adam Claytor
Jahna Harris	Matthew Seward
Uncle Mark Barbour	Odis Parker
Uncle Sean Coats	Currecia Coleman
Maria Caminiti	Camille Francis
Lewis Howes	Elizabeth Williams
Wolfe Starr	Nick Zizi
Miara Pack	Clarence Washington
Tiara Pack	Kelvin Collins
Aunty Betty Pack	Tiffanie Tillman
Unc Charles	Jeffrey Gitomer

Shene Brownlee

Mike Mehrle

Terrence Shelton

Robert Smith

Jaja Stoudemire

Yusif Sadiq

Gerry Hammond

T.C.

Pastor Tyus

Dr. Bishop Derrick Reeves

Karen Owens

Table of Contents

Connect & Grow *Rich*

Preface

My mother called me up the steps one day. What could she want? Clean out the tub, make your bed, flush the toilet; nothing seemed out of the ordinary. None of the above. In her right hand she held a pink plastic comb. Wide mouthed with maybe 2 teeth visible. The remaining unseen teeth were being hidden by a thick layer of coarse black hair. In her left hand was a small mirror with which she had apparently been using to see the rear parts of her head that reflected from the mirror above the sink. I reached out to touch the ancillary device in her hand still not understanding what the contents of its possession would mean to me. Seeing the look in my eye and the slight relaxation in my lower jaw, she first removed the tuft of hair from the comb and then began to move the comb back towards her head. In one fell swoop, she plowed the teeth again through her thick locks only to reveal a lonely patch of unfertile land. Swoop, again. Another bald spot. And then again. And then again. I could now plainly see the

majority of my mother's follicle-less head. My head lowered
as I could feel the rivers begin to flow from deep inside me.
My mother was sick. She was sick, and her son had not given
her the life and the freedom he had promised her. I was sick.
Gently, she lifted my chin and looked in my eyes. "Terryll"
(my middle name, only used by close family and friends) she
said, "Don't be sad. If I'm losing this head of hair, it's because
God meant for me to have a better grade of hair, so I have to
get rid of this first".

In other words, what my mother said to me was, where we
go in life is determined by this singular truth: It's not what
happens to us in life. It's how we react to what happens to us.

As I descended down the steps I couldn't help but observe
the cohesive flow of color between the carpet and the wall. 26
years years of coming back and forth to the house I grew up
in and it had never stood out before. Strange, how when your
life changes, so does your perspective of it.

This was to be only the first of many trials I would encounter
in the ensuing months pending my mother's cancer diagnosis.
Slowly and methodically my life began to take somewhat of
a downward spiral. What I found interesting is the number of
people that supported me and held me up in the light of my
hardest times. I wrote this book in a period of my life where
all I had were my dreams and my connections.

Those same connections are the sole reason
that this book was able to be completed.

There are a couple of reasons that I was insistent on finishing this book. First and foremost is due to the fact that I made the commitment to all the friends in my social network to do it… something a month after I started I would wish I wouldn't have ever done! Secondly I had one of my closest friends (Jamal Dorsey, R.I.P) that I grew up with die in a tragic car accident at the tender age of 29 years old. He believed in me sometimes more than I believed in myself and I told him I would have it done before Christmas of '09. He left and now is in a better place but his death brought me to a realization: life is short and when I leave here, I should leave something that will be here long after I am gone.

Introduction

Let's keep it real. For most people, including myself, the word
networking has a negative connotation. In fact, I'm pretty
sure I have N.A.D.D.: Networking Attention Deficit Disorder.
Going to networking events and staying the whole time is a
pretty grueling task for me. Getting 30 business cards shoved
in my hand by people that only look at me as a dollar sign is
not necessarily my idea of emotional advancement. Typically,
after I get home and pull the stack of cards out of my pocket,
that practically all look the same to me now, I put them in my
drawer where the other hundreds of cards have been put to
rest.

To be honest, it wasn't until I was halfway through writing
this book that I found that because the word sounds watered
down doesn't mean there's not power still in it. If you can get
by the fact that after you graduate from college, everything
you go to will be called a "networking" event, you will be just
fine.

The goal of this book is to teach you how to become rich. Not just rich as in terms of your financial bank account, but more so in terms of your emotional bank account, i.e. rich with connections. Therefore, being rich by this definition is being wealthy as an individual internally, as opposed to the material things that make up external wealth. Rich relationships, or *connection-ships* as I call them, will take you to places faster and more effortlessly than you ever dreamed. Even if you are an introvert or someone that just seems to repel people away from you, having the right connections will show you how to make the most out of every interaction and overcome rejection, fear, self-doubt and low self esteem.

I will show you simple, yet effective and precise ways to attain connections that, if cared for properly, will lead you to happiness, fulfillment, and wealth.

Throughout this journey I will show you:

- How to build lifelong relationships with friends, customers, bosses, and business partners that lead to getting more done in less time.

- How to double your business in 5 days with one single principle

- How to memorize people's name within 5 seconds of initial introduction

- How to become an expert at reading body

language. Only 7% of people of professionals know how to use these skills.

- How to connect with the most powerful people in any profession regardless of your current status or position

- How to maneuver to engage any person you come in contact with

- How to utilize the Power of Asking to get whatever you want.

- How to effectively connect so you don't waste your time like 95% of common "networkers"

- How to establish yourself as the high-value contact that your colleagues can't afford not to know.

In addition, I will show you how to create the law of attraction, and begin invoking the type of relationships that you do not simply tolerate, but thoroughly enjoy.

At the end of each chapter there is a blank page. Take the time and write notes. A short pencil is better than a long memory!

Bottom line: I will show you how to tap into the richest resource in the planet – *People*.

Chapter 1

*A Connectionaire
Is Born*

"THERE IS ALWAYS ONE
MOMENT IN CHILDHOOD
WHEN THE DOOR OPENS
AND LETS THE FUTURE IN."

- DEEPAK CHOPRA

Redefined

It's important that you know where I come from, what I've seen and what I've done. It's also important for you to get a better understanding of the concepts you will be learning in this book. Throughout the course of your reading, I will attempt to be as transparent as possible because one thing I want you to walk away with from reading this book, more than anything, is the knowledge that everything that has ever been done, is possible for you to do, and what's even better is that there is an entire world of things that have not been done that we are waiting on you to accomplish.

My career, in a sense, began with networking, so in this chapter, this is where we also will begin. Let's define a few terms first.

Main Entry: **net·work·ing**
Function: *verb*
the exchange of information or services among individuals, groups, or institutions; specifically: the cultivation of productive relationships for employment or business

Between 1967 and the present, the term networking has morphed into something almost unrecognizable compared to its original meaning. The word *networking* sounds like the one thing that most people hate doing: working.

Often, people believe networking is swapping business cards at a Chamber of Commerce meeting. You may attend a company's event on Facebook or in a local conference room, and it's dubbed a "networking" event. Here's a dirty little secret – if it starts after eight or nine on the weekends, all it's going to be is a meet and greet or a party.

> Main Entry: **con·nect**
> Function: *verb*
> ***1. to have or establish a rapport***
> ***2. the development process of finding, cultivating, nurturing and building relationships.***

Connecting is based on the sharing of common ground. Common ground is based on people, places and things. And the more common ground you have with someone, the higher the trust level. The higher the trust level, the more willingness the person has to share key contacts, information and resources. See the connection?

The difference between networking and connecting is like the difference between memorization and studying in school. Memorization will get you an "A" on the quiz. Studying will help you pass the finals. When you think about it, connecting is the Ph.D. of networking. It's the next step, the graduate level. In networking, it's the handshake and the smile. But connecting is all about the heartfelt emotion and the trust.

It's the exciting burst of energy that sparks when you meet someone who shares your values, and can add value or just takes interest by questioning your reasoning and challenging you. The person who does this isn't trying to be a millionaire. He will have more than a rich bank account. He will have a richer life.

Main Entry: **con·nec·tion·aire**

> Function: *noun*
> *1. a person who builds wealth through creating personal connections as opposed to capital gain*
>
> *2. a person who can be fiscally deficient, yet still receive V.I.P. treatment due to his extensive network of influential contacts*
>
> *3. someone who establishes life-long relationships and builds his personal brand into a wealth of indeterminable value*

For all you spelling bee champions and wordsmiths out there, I know you're thinking to yourself; "I've never seen that word in the dictionary before"! Well, you're right. I would love to tell you about how I traveled to Shangri La and spoke to the Shaman's of never ending wisdom and they prophesied over my life and my destiny imploring me to give the world "The Connectionaire", or about the fireside chat I had with Barack Obama and Warren Buffet, where Ivan Misner jokingly dubbed me The Connectionaire, and the name just stuck with me, or how it floated down to me on a cloud as I led the masses out the doors of the networking conference and into the promised land…but none of that would be true.

The truth is, I was at my computer one night, working late as usual (or early, as it was about 2 in the morning) and thinking about the direction I was going with my business. At the time I didn't know specifically what I was doing, I just knew that I love helping people connect. Bridging gaps just seemed to collapse time frames, and if I could help people skip a few steps in the connection process it seemed like it would make a lot of sense. I mean, why not? I would be providing people with a more practical solution, and in turn I would be satisfying my personal purpose. They could have more time to spend with family or for travel, and at the end of the day I will have done something worthwhile. Sounded like the perfect plan, but the question became, what would I call myself and how do I begin to build my personal brand?

I began bouncing a few names around. My first thought was "The Connector" but I quickly conceded that it sounded more like a TBS mini-series and honestly was just downright corny. In addition, I had heard it used before. I decided that I needed something new, something that had been previously unheard or hadn't even been thought of. The word millionaire has always been exceptionally attractive to me and I was sure many others felt the same, so I thought that was a good place to start. The word in itself embodied everything that I wanted to represent financially, but I had to find a way to give it a meaning more relevant to my message of building value by building relationships. I had to display the relevance of connecting. It took about 20 minutes of rolling it around in my head before it hit me! Connect, Millionaire, Connect, Millionaire, Connect, Millionaire. Connectionaire!

I then had to justify the word to myself before I could teach

it as a lifestyle. I had met a number of millionaires in my life, but was I connecting people to them? At the time, not really. I evaluated the word millionaire again and found a Wikipedia entry that defined a millionaire as a person who was very rich in value. That to me became the distinguishable difference in becoming a Connectionaire. A millionaire is rich in value, a Connectionaire is valuable in spite of his riches. This is a person who seeks to enrich the lives of others, in his/her community, and throughout the world. If one has an abundance of funds in his/her bank account yet dies never having touched anyone else's life, what has he really accomplished? But if I've helped an abundance of people regardless of the status of my financial portfolio, then I have been truly valuable. And that is the essence of leaving a legacy.A connectionaire is a person who has developed wealth through his connections rather than money. He can walk into a place without a dime in his pocket and still receive rock star treatment because of how well he is connected to every person in the room. He focuses on building lifelong relationships and adding value first. He considers himself a servant, and understands where and how he is in a position to help, and is ecstatically willing to do so.

Lesson 1: Trust under the razor

The first thing you need to know is that you are **Special**. Not **special** in the sense that your mother consoles you with when you're down or facing trials, but absolutely like no other person on the planet. The word special is defined as such:

Having a specific or particular purpose, function, etc.;

***distinguished or different from what is ordinary or usual;
extraordinary; exceptional as in amount of degree.***

Every man or woman is born with a particular set of skills in a particular set of circumstances that makes us truly unique. Whatever it is that you were born to do; only you can do it. Knowing this is what will give you the confidence to make the connections that will improve your life and your career. The *trick* is: finding that thing that sets you apart from everyone else. The *clue* is: the secret almost always lies in something you've already been doing, something you love, and something that people who know you already recognize you for. For me, it was making connections. And my first example of this ability came at an early age… when I needed a haircut.

You know when you see the cover of Ebony magazine, and on it there's that suave, debonair, super-cool looking brother, with the award winning smile? Well that guy was not me. In fact, I was probably the complete opposite of that guy. I have two brothers and two sisters. 5 kids in 1 house and I fit somewhere in the middle. Between extra-curricular activities and two working parents there was rarely enough time to get me to the barbershop. However, my parents were gracious enough to give me $5 and send me to the local barber *college*, where barbers go to learn their trade. In a barber college, there are three different levels of barbers: beginner, intermediate and advanced. Service prices are in accordance with the rank of the barber, and $5 meant a mid-level cut. These were guys that had been studying but had limited haircutting experience; and it showed.

Seeing my malcontent with the current system of cosmetic

conversion, and needing to find a way to cut a few corners financially, my mom eventually purchased her own set of clippers. From then on I was graced with the "chili bowl" haircut. She literally put a blue plastic cereal bowl on my head and cut around it. This furthered served to increase my notoriety at school. Acne and the "chili bowl" lent themselves nicely to my already struggling self-confidence. What should be noted here is that I never accepted the status quo. I never let a circumstance or a lack of resource dictate what my ultimate outcome could be.

Aware I needed to take control of my situation; I took the clippers and started cutting my own hair. I set out on the course of mastering my craft one trim at a time. Oh sure, I was bald a couple hundred times, but eventually I got the hang of it. No longer the laughing stock (at least not in reference to my hair) I was able to convince a few of my friends to let me cut their hair. As it turns out, I had a talent. People started to notice my skills improving and soon enough, at the age of 12, I had a small business. I was charging anywhere from $1 or $2 up to about $7 to a clientele range that included high school students and even teachers!

I want you to walk away with a couple of lessons from my experience, and these are things that should always stay with you.

There was one key principle that my business helped me understand: how to build and maintain relationships. I learned that arguably the most important aspect of a relationship is trust. Trust is imperative each time a person sits down in my chair, as their appearances, as well as reputation are in my

hands. In building business relationships you have to start with trust. A great way to gain that trust is by being attentive to what people talk about.

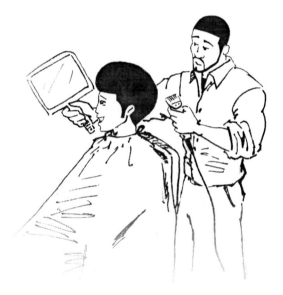

Listening is a major factor in building relationships. Most people enjoy talking about what they know and offering their opinions. By tuning in to others, I would come up with a lot of ideas and was even offered different opportunities. I'm not going to say that *every time* you listen you will gain personal benefits. But, mastering this skill shows people that you care and allows them to be more honest and open. It was building the right relationships with the right people and learning to listen that got me many of my successes.

Recognizing the positive in spite of the negative...

Knowing your value is what will help other people recognize value in you.

College Days

I'm going to make a simple statement: Where I am in my life can mostly be attributed to the connection I have made along the way.

I served my collegiate tenure at Wright State University, but I received my education long before I arrived on campus. What I learned prior to achieving the ranks of the scholarly was that average could not be my standard. I was serving people long before I got to college; literally. I worked at every restaurant establishment in Columbus Ohio. My first paying, federally filed job was at McDonald's when I was 16 years old. The man who owned the McDonalds where I got my first job was a member of the church I grew up in, and a family friend. My father told him I was looking to work and I'm pretty positive I didn't even fill out an application. As appreciative as I was for the opportunity, I quickly moved up to more lucrative ventures such as Wendy's, Panera Bread, Johnny Rockets, PF Chang, etc. Suffice to say; when I got to college, I knew I had to find a more effective way to make a living. For me, working 60 hours a week for a couple hundred dollars wasn't going to cut it.

Fortunately, I still had my high school trade to fall back on, and by that time my haircuts were looking great. I decided that I wanted take a stab at barbering as a career. I was in shape from playing sports in high school and my acne had finally cleared up. To round it out, a couple of years and a couple ounces of metal had cleared up a slight orthodontic issue. I had created an image for myself. That image would be instrumental if I were to be able to make a successful

run at the local barber crown. There were a handful of other barbers that were at Wright State so I knew I would have to be strategic if I wanted to make cutting hair my main job at school and not another restaurant.

My first priority was to devise a clear strategy. I decided to put some simple logic to work; I had to make my product the most visible, and the most appealing. Give a man something free, and you have a friend, or a customer, for life. Mark Cuban once said if you anger your crowd; just deploy the free t-shirt tactic. To attract new customers, I offered the first haircut free. Taking it a step further, I also gave the customer their next cut for only $5. The worst barber at that time was charging $7 so I made my prices lower than everyone else and provided a superior service at the same time. Living in a quad (a room for 4 people) on campus gave me the advantage of being visible to a seemingly endless stream of college students that could become clients. Through this system I was able to make a reasonable amount of money in my freshman year of college.

My plan was successful for the most part, accomplishing both of my objectives, and took me comfortably to the end of the school year. I was making consistent money, but not the kind of income that would allow me to reach any of my long term goals. In addition, I had become grossly popular in light of my trade.

As fate would have it, I caught a big break entering into my sophomore year at Wright State. I had already upped my prices from $5 to $7 as I was no longer "fresh meat", and I quickly set out to establish myself in my new domain. My

new dorm allocation landed me in another quad, but this one was a major step up from my previous living arrangement. I was placed in College Park, a housing unit that hosted a majority of juniors and seniors. My roommates here were all popular of their own, one of whom was the most renowned DJ in Dayton, OH. Friends of his would become friends of mine and soon after they would become clients. I also employed another principle that was pertinent in gaining repeat customers; I never compromised the standard of my services. I was very particular about the quality of the haircut my customers received and I kept my prices competitive so my clients always left with a sense of increased and fair value.

Being dedicated and creating strong relationships opened up other doors for me as well. I began participating in hair shows where I would display "Cutz by Coats" in a runway style fashion show. This garnered yet more exposure which translated to more clients and more money. Yet, I still wasn't able to reach my desired level of financial stability. I continued to search for ways to improve my business and income potential, and then I received a phone call that would set me in a completely different direction.

The call came from a high school friend named John Toy. He informed me that he had become involved with a company and that they were looking to expand. Without reluctance I agreed to meet with his manager to learn more about the company. What I was introduced to was the world of network marketing.

For the few of you who may not be familiar with this system of business, network marketing is a structure that relies on

a viral system of placing additional entrepreneurs into a pyramid style setting with one person at the top and unlimited people stagnated beneath him/her. That person then becomes the top of their own "tree", adding to the number of people that links all the way back to the original person. Prior to this encounter I had no idea there was anything of this magnitude available for me to explore. The unquestionable and unlimited potential for my financial growth was immediately apparent to me and I jumped on the opportunity without hesitation. I began sharing the information with others who in turn would tell others. Within 5 months I was making $5,000 in a month! That was the most I had ever made in my life! 5 months later I make over $10,000 in a month and all this while I'm still attending classes at Wright State. In no time at all, I had abandoned the dorm room for my own apartment and was spending a little time at the dealership buying new cars. I was finally living the lifestyle that I had envisioned for myself. Working in network marketing also made me privy to a vast ocean of entrepreneurs and great business intellects that I was able to build friendships with. My relationships with many people across the country landed me on expense-paid flights to different places throughout the state just to socialize. My hotels, food and pretty much every other expense would be taken care of. Through good standing relationships, trust, and reliability, I was able to find success in my career as well as my personal life.

Allow me to back track for a moment here and make one point clear to you. There were a couple of things that I had going for me which I would use to my advantage. I worked hard and I built relationships. What I did not have, was any

particular set of hard skills that allowed me to be wildly successful. I was not the best speaker or motivator, I was simply showing people a good product and because they believed in me, they believed in what I told them. I did not party or go to basketball games or date frivolously. Almost every dollar I made I invested back into the business and into myself though personal development. Even the expensive cars I enjoyed were more so an extension of the image I wanted to project. My biggest benefit was surrounding myself with other people who were extremely successful. By my junior year I had amassed a huge network at Wright State, and I used that to my advantage as well. Think about it, I was cutting 7-10 heads a day while in school and I was pretty popular so when it came time for me to introduce others to what I was doing all I did was tell them to take a look at what I was doing. If they liked it, great, if not, then that was good too. It didn't matter if not everyone bought into the system, the possibilities were still endless.

That experience taught me it's not *what* you know, but *who* you know. In business, you need simply to know the *why* and the *how* will reveal its self later. Through your connections, you will be able to go to the right people to figure out the *how*. Such is the importance of building a lasting relationship.

Later I would reflect on two concepts. If one phone call could open the doors to a more profitable future for me, what other opportunities could be on the horizon? If my network and friendships could be so revolutionary for me, then who could I open doors for?

Action Steps for Chapter 1:

• Write down 3 ways you can take control of your current situation to make it better.

————————————————————

————————————————————

————————————————————

————————————————————

• Write down 20 of the names that come to mind first and that you have good relationships with (regardless of whether they're in your industry or niche). Now write down the people that you WANT to know most. Ask the people you know if they have contacts that could connect you with the people you WANT to know.

• Define your Niche- Remember Prosperity Follows Passion. Narrow it down to one thing, and then look for people that are already doing what you want to do.

• Set up one appointment a week with a contact that you have made and find ways that you can give him/her value first

Take Away Lessons from Chapter 1:

✓ Listen. Some of the world's best opportunities come to those who keep their mouths shut.

✓ Be a connectionaire. Start adding value first with those people who are really there for you and not what they can get out of you.

✓ Tune out of WIIFM (What's In It For Me) and tune into WCID4U (What Can I Do For You)!

✓ Don't keep score. You'll lose in the end.

<u>NOTES</u>

Chapter 2

Fear, Lies and Sabotage!

"LET GO OF THE THINGS YOU FEAR TO LOSE. DIE TO YOUR ATTACHMENTS. FREE YOURSELF FROM EVERYTHING YOU THINK YOU ARE AND EMBRACE THE TRUTH THAT YOU ARE ABUNDANT, ETERNAL, FEARLESS AND WORTH BEING LOVED."

- MASTIN KIPP

The journey to success begins with self-confidence. You must first believe you can achieve your goal. In other words: If you think you're going to fail, you will. When you exude doubtfulness other people also pick up on it. When you exude confidence, passion, and positive energy others will latch onto that and doors will open for you!

Love Yourself First & What You Do

Love is the strongest emotion that we have. At the core, love is what makes us do nearly everything that we do. As a young man, probably the single most significant reason I always wanted to be rich is so I could take care of my parents. Now that's love! More than anything since I started my entrepreneurial journey in my teens my goal was to make enough to take care of my mother and father and then lastly myself.

Love comes with a certain duality to it. Meaning, you have to not only love what you do but you have to love yourself. I

know when you hear certain things or when you hear people say, "You have to love yourself", you kind of cringe but in all honestly you absolutely do, and I mean that in the most masculine way possible!

When you have love for yourself not only do you treat others better but you also protect yourself, because you create a standard on how other people are going to treat you. Remember the saying, "Looking for love in all the wrong places..."? In order to negate that statement, you first have to look at yourself.

Bernie Mac one of the most famous comedians of this era tells a story about how he started his career. He said one day he saw his mother crying so he went over and sat on her lap and asked her, "Mom, why are you crying"? She replied, "No reason son..." Noticing that his mother's attention was focused elsewhere he realized that he heard Bill Cosby speaking on the T.V. in the background. Moments later he witnessed his mother laughing and crying at the same time. He in turn also started laughing and immediately had an "aha" moment. He proclaimed to his mother, "Mom, I'm going to be a comedian, so I never have to see you cry again!"

Recognize your F.E.A.R.

Fear is as natural of an emotion as love, anger, or excitement. You will face things in your life that will make you afraid or

nervous. There are no 2 ways around it. What most of us fail to realize is that we have an option in how we respond to that fear. We can look at fear in one of 2 ways. We can look at F.E.A.R. and *Forget Everything Appearing **Rough*** or we can look at F.E.A.R. as an opportunity to Face Everything And Recover. Jeffrey Gitomer describes the roots of fear in three individual categories:

1. Lack of Preparation
2. Rejection
3. Limited self-image/self-esteem

Sufficient preparation is imperative if you are to accurately and efficiently engage a soon-to-be connection. Let's look at preparation another way; let's call it *proof of belief*. You don't really believe in what you're doing until you've taken the time to study, practice and develop it.

Author and entrepreneur Eben Pagan documents an idea of where the fear of rejection emanates from. He states:

"Rejection by another human being triggers a part of the brain, a pain center in the brain that is the same center that physical pain triggers. So, rejection by a person actually hurts the same way that physical pain hurts."
– Eben Pagan

What you need to become is a master of continuing in spite of the pain. We all encounter situations in life that can look like a road block, when in reality they are merely speed bumps, train tracks, or often times, bridges. You need to go over, go under, or go through these obstacles instead of stopping. A major key to be able to accomplish this is to attach a big enough vision of why you are going to succeed and how you are going to get there that it will force you to act in spite of the fear. Your vision is your road map to where you want to be. When you understand the significance of your vision, you can begin to understand the necessity for the ups and downs along the process so that you may face them courageously.

Your courage is an ever-evolving extension of you. Learn to give yourself every opportunity for that courage to grow. Surround yourself with people who speak to the king or queen in you rather than the coward. Your growth as an individual is as vital as your growth as a professional. One typically doesn't happen without the other. This is the power of building strong connections. By surrounding yourself with people that seek to advance themselves, they will also seek to advance you, and vice versa.

Perception of self is usually the definitive factor. The popular word for the necessary attribute is *swagger*. I'll stick with a more recognizable term and call it confidence. It shows in

your walk, and in how you speak. It is related in your smile and felt in your presence the moment you enter a room. In connecting, you must know that you are the one that should be sought after. You must present yourself as if failure does not exist. What would you do if you knew you couldn't fail? The key is to believe is if that is exactly what the truth is. Whether you think you can, or you think you can't, you're right.

Find Your Inner Kanye

If everyone believed in themselves as much as Kanye West, we'd be a lot further then where we are now. Kanye West is a huge rapper, and business mogul. You may know him best from his "George Bush doesn't like black people" comment or the Taylor Swift incident at the VMA awards. A lot of people may not like him but something you can't say about him is that he doesn't believe in his self. As a matter of fact the first thing you may say is, "I don't like him because he's too cocky or arrogant." I believe that that exact trait is why he's gone as far as he has today!

In college I heard him say on his first cd "I can let these dream killers, kill my self esteem or use my arrogance as esteem to power my dream, I use it as my gas so they say that I'm gassed but without it I'd be last so I ought to laugh!" Kanye is not afraid because he is being himself. If somebody doesn't like it then oh well. This is me. Love it or hate it. Take it or leave it.

When I first started my journey being a young entrepreneur the people closest to me said that I would fail. They didn't mean this with bad attentions they just didn't want me to get hurt. But I let that ignite a fire in me because I love proving people wrong. The greatest adversary to failure is massive success. When I got into network marketing I heard a million reasons why I shouldn't waste my time. "It's a scam", "no one makes money like that", "It's a pyramid scheme", and so on. I took a risk and did it and after less than a year while I was in college I was making more money than my professors. I got over my fear of rejection and speaking in front of people. I had mentors for the first time in my life who gave me valuable information and some of them were millionaires. I had never spoken to millionaires before that. I started reading books and then fell in love with reading, devouring almost 1 book a week. Most important it was the first time I went against the grain and it gave me even more fuel to trust my own instincts.

When you find your inner Kanye, no matter what negative

comments people make you will be impenetrable. Most importantly, you can take control and be the person you want to be, not what someone else wants you to be.

"Don't be afraid to be you, the ORIGINAL you. Not a copycat version of someone else."

The Greatest fear people have is that of being themselves. They want to be this celebrity or that star. They do what everyone else does and that doesn't fit where and who they are. But you get nowhere that way; your energy is weak and no one pays attention to you. You're running away from the one thing that you own—your unique talent that gives you your individuality.

"I lost that fear, and once I felt the power that I felt by showing the world I didn't care about being like other people, I could never go back"
– 50 Cent

What are the lies we believe?

(1) I'm not a people person, so I can't connect with people
(2) I'm not skilled enough to connect
(3) I don't know or like talking to people I don't know
(4) I don't want to appear nerdy or helpless
(5) I don't have anything of value to give
(6) I don't have a job or business yet, so I can't
(7) I might fail

Belief is the first thing to change people's lives, but the last place people look. Your inner-self creates your external appearance. If you don't believe in yourself other people won't. Take the time to work on your inner connections.

What controls the decisions you will make in your life? Is it your surroundings? Your friends, your family, your upbringing? Perhaps your level of intelligence (or the lack thereof)... Or, is it your beliefs?

Anthony Robbins compares the human mind to a kitchen table. In his audio book, Awaken the Giant Within You, he speculates that thoughts are a table top and the things that build your table are the legs, which are references (References here meaning lessons, experiences, and visual interpretations). When you get 3 or more references that *you* make up for yourself, whether they are real or totally made up (because your subconscious mind can't differentiate between what's real and what is fake), you combine your reference with a thought and poof!... You have a belief! To make it plain, a belief is simply an extreme certainty.

The Peanut and the Spider Monkey

The spider monkey is considered a new age monkey. This simply means that this breed of monkey is underdeveloped with a smaller intelligence capacity than the traditional monkeys

we learn about in school. South American hunters prey on the spider monkey. By nature, spider monkeys are protective and defensive which makes them difficult to corral. In order to avoid fighting the elusive mammal, the hunters instead choose to trap them. Using a heavy container with a small opening in the top, and a wide bottom, the hunter strategically drops his lure. The bait: a special nut that is irresistible to the spider monkey. After the hunter has disappeared, the monkey will come down from his treetop hideaway, attracted by the scent of the nut. The monkey reaches into the container, his flexible hand barely fitting inside. Now here's the kicker, once the monkey clenches the nut in his palm, his hand is too big to be removed from the container, and the container is too heavy to be carried away. Defeated, the monkey, instead of simply letting go of the nut, will sit down and hold on to the nut still inside of the container. The hunter has only to pick up the monkey and carry it away to its demise.

Now some of you are wondering why the stupid monkey doesn't just let the peanut go. I ask you the same question:

Are you happy with your life right now or are you holding onto the same peanut beliefs that will leave you broke… not just financially broke, but also emotionally or worse yet, spiritually bankrupt?

You can place blame on other people, or situations, or

circumstances, but you never take a step back and look at the common denominator... YOU!

The truth is, perhaps that your beliefs and your perception of self is simply distorted. You believe that the life you currently lead is all that you deserve. You do the same things because it's all that you know. Einstein says that doing the same thing over and over and expecting different results is insanity. So what you have to do is change the way that you believe.

Begin by questioning your current set of beliefs. Identify the things in your life that are holding you back and try to evaluate the connection these setbacks have to your belief system. Search to find the "3 references" that have solidified these beliefs in your head. Keep a close eye on your "intake". The things that we see, hear, and feel are directly related to what we believe. If you want to reshape what you believe, change what you take in to your mind.

Destroy Limiting Beliefs

Limiting Beliefs are the beliefs that are keeping you from attaining or accomplishing what you really want. The beliefs that tell you that if you're successful then people will resent you, they'll no longer truly love you for who you are, only for what you have. That if you are getting wealth that it's taking away from someone or that it's better to be meek because you have a better chance of getting into heaven. It could simply be

the belief that you can't have successful relationships if you are a mega-success.

You can't generalize that everyone is like that or that this is the singular outcome of your success. Fear is what made people teach you these things and you made an agreement that they were true. It's time to break all the beliefs that do not absolutely empower you.

Take an inventory of all your beliefs and see what is holding you back.

Finally; you have to stop beating yourself up! Stop believing the lies or deceptive agreements that were made up for you before you were old enough to make your own decisions, or that you created yourself. This way of thinking is only a prison that will hold you hostage until you are ready to let it go. Never believe that what is in your hand is more valuable than the life you could have if you simply opened it up.

The belief you have about yourself and the world of "networking" are things that guide you. If your belief is that people who network are always trying to sell things, and you do not want to take part, you will attract only these experiences with networking. A belief becomes reality. Beliefs give you tunnel-vision, so it is up to you to focus on the positive.

*"To conquer oneself is a greater victory
than to conquer thousands in battle."*
—Buddha

Action Steps from Chapter 2:

- Take a minute to look at yourself in the mirror right now. Is that the face, clothing, and attitude of a world class business owner? What actions do you need to take right now to change that?

- What *would* you do if you knew you couldn't fail? Take a few minutes to ponder that thought with closed eyes. Then write your response down on paper. Now turn that idea into your own action steps and create the success you've always wanted!

Take Away Lessons from Chapter 2:

✓ If you can't believe in yourself, no one else will. Really concentrate on building and growing something you're proud to put your name on!

✓ Don't allow the lies of small-thinkers to belittle your dreams. If the success you desire was impossible, no one would ever have achieved it before! Bill Gates has billions of dollars! Warren Buffet has created an empire from being the lowest paid CEO in the world. Your dreams and successes are a direct result of what YOU want them to be!

✓ You become what you think about most. Concentrate on success!

Connect & Grow *Rich*

<u>NOTES</u>

Chapter 3

*Become Friends With
The Angel Of Death...
Carpe Diem*

"LIVE THIS DAY AS IF IT WILL
BE YOUR LAST REMEMBER
THAT YOU WILL ONLY
FIND TOMORROW ON THE
CALENDAR OF FOOLS. FORGET
YESTERDAYS DEFEATS AND
IGNORE THE PROBLEMS
OF TOMORROW. THIS IS IT!
DOOMSDAY. ALL YOU HAVE.
MAKE IT THE BEST DAY OF
YOUR YEAR. TAKE THE BATON,
NOW. RUN WITH IT! THIS IS
YOUR DAY!"

- OG MANDINO

Resources are all around us. More often than not, our greatest resource is the first one we overlook. It is often easy for us to "over-think" our positions and "over-evaluate" the things that are necessary. In business, what becomes most important is simply; *taking action*. This is one of the reasons that this book is littered with *Action Steps* in every chapter. One must always plan and remain conscious of the plan and the goals that are laid out by that plan, but the all important step is: taking the first step! When you commit to taking action, you will bear witness to the myriad of resources that become available to you.

One of my students approached me after one of my recent Connect Your Life events and asked me, "Hey Rob, what's the best connecting story you've ever had?" After a moment of thought I told him, the truth is, the best thing that's happened as a result of my connections was in my ability to help someone else.

This is the story I told him:

Ryan's Story

While visiting my younger brother; he showed me a letter he received from the National Dean's List. The letter explained he was in the top one-half percent of college students in the country. It went on to read that he'd been offered a chance to go to three different countries across the globe and represent the United States. However it cost $8,000 to go and it was his responsibility to raise the money. The nail in the coffin was that the deadline to sign up was a week from that day. He needed to have the full $8,000 within 30 days in order to go.

He never thought about going, because he didn't have the finances. My parents were extremely supportive even though there was nothing they could do financially to assist him. They never lost faith that 'something could happen'.

Reading the letter, I saw words like "*opportunity of a lifetime*", and to "*meet with and make connections with people from Harvard*". He would be able to meet and study under some of the top CEOs of Fortune 500 companies.

He had this amazing gift and was just going to let it pass him by! What bothered me was the fact that he was so nonchalant about it. He didn't really think or believe he could really go. He was ready to pack it away and say, "Oh, okay, well here's the letter. This is evidence that I'll put on my wall as proof that I could've done something great, and I'll have it to show

to my grandkids someday and say, 'Hey, look at what I had a chance to do, this is how good I was'."

I remembered a quote by ancient Chinese philosopher, Lao Tzu: "The wise man does not lay up his own treasurers; the more he gives to others, the more he has for his own." This piece of wisdom applied to my brother, as he was sitting on a treasure that could open doors for himself and many others behind him, yet was perfectly willing to let the opportunity pass him by, but it also had great meaning to me in this moment. I knew it would be as much my failure as his if I sat back and allowed him to crumple up this page in his life, and throw it over his shoulder.

There was NO WAY I could let my brother pass up on an opportunity like this. We had one day until the deadline to sign up. I made the $500 deposit within 5 minutes of reading the letter and instructed my brother to run to the post office and get the letter in as fast as he could.

Five hundred dollars down, seventy-five hundred to go. I began to contemplate on my options for creating the remainder of the necessary funds to send my brother on his trip. At the time, I was a mortgage broker. There were up and down months in that industry. Sometimes the down months stretched to 7 or 8 months at a time. It wasn't likely I would land a large enough commission to pay for it out of pocket

and I didn't have the 9 to 5 job that my brother needed me to have in order to make the full payment for his trip either.

We needed a miracle. So being a Christian man, I prayed for one. I remember praying that night, crying and saying "God he's an example. He's so good. He's done so many things right. He's so disciplined. If You have to, take away my blessings for a while, just so he can go on this trip! It will change his life. He's going to meet so many people there. He's going to connect with so many people. It'll give him more belief in the future if he has a dream!"

Then I immediately went to work, I reached out and connected with 7 of my friends and created a plan.

The One Dollar Dream

Seven friends; one mission – help my brother raise $7,500.

We were faced with a couple of initial hurdles. Time, which we had practically none to spare, and experience; none of us had been in the position to raise such a seemingly large amount of money in such a short period of time.

Reaching out to our known resources, we asked another friend of ours in Chicago to create a website. Nothing too intricate, just something simple that would suit our purpose. So the site was being created, but it needed a name. It had

to be something that was immediately representative of our purpose but also catchy enough to draw interest and create curiosity. The site being still in its fledgling stages, the priority of naming it took a back seat to another important detail; the plan itself.

We decided that the most sufficient route to take was to get the community involved. Make this effort their own and get people to donate to the cause. I thought, "What is an amount that everybody can give?" And the first thing that came to my head was a dollar. My thinking was that most people, even if you approached a complete stranger and said, "Oh excuse me. You wouldn't happen to have a dollar on you", would give you a dollar without even thinking twice! It was an amount that was feasible for everyone.

One dollar to help my brother achieve a dream, and the name was set. We called it **The One Dollar Dream**! We knew that if we could get enough people to give one dollar, or even more, we could raise enough money.

The Viral Explosion

The plan was simple, yet very effective. First, we created little neon green business cards that were really, really ugly that said "The One Dollar Dream, tell a friend". They were ugly, but unmistakable and unforgettable. This was important because it gave our cause immediate recognition. Everyone

knew the One Dollar Dream business card when they saw it.

Next, we changed all of our Facebook pages to a photo image of *The One Dollar Dream* flier. We also prompted other friends to change their Facebook picture to the same image. This added to our online visibility, using the advantage of a large social network as leverage to reach out to more people.

In addition, we recorded my brother speaking (and quite passionately I might add) in his own words about the magnitude of the opportunity that he had been presented. This served to give our cause a face and a more tangible representation that would-be contributors could attach their emotions to.

We accepted physical donations in person and also had a PayPal button added to the website where people could go online and donate.

...And in the process of less than a month, we were able to raise *$10,000!*

That was more than enough money for my brother to go on the trip, and even have a little spending money! My brother was able to go on the trip and create memories and experiences that will carry him for the rest of his life. Now he can tell his grand children one day about what he did, instead of telling them about what he could have done.

It was a life changing experience for me also as it allowed me and the friends that helped me to bring this dream to a reality to come closer together, and it was all because of the power of our connections. The interesting lesson that I was able to learn from this experience is that when you reach out for help, the ones who respond will not always be the ones you'd expect. The money didn't come from the folks who could have easily paid for the entire trip. Not even from churches that could have taken up a donation or love offering. We got all the money from people that were either broke, or were middle or lower class with barely anything to spare. They were the

ones who said, "Hey, I believe in that cause. I know I don't know you, but here you go. Here's $5, here's $10, here's $20." That's how we raised the money.

The largest donation came from my sister; a single mother rearing two boys. She'd just gotten her tax refund of $1,000, and she signed over the entire check for to him to go on the trip.

Action Steps from Chapter 3:

- Your dream is dead in the water without a plan. Sit down right now and create 3 Action Steps you can take immediately to start working on your own goals in life. Be specific!

- There were two very important reasons we were able to get Ryan the money he needed. First, was the use of social networking websites. Facebook allows you to have a maximum of 5,000 members. Have you maxed out your friends yet? Request new friends daily to maximize the number of eyes that see what you're offering!

- The second important reason we were successful was the use of friends and family. The one's you hold dearest want to see you succeed. Don't hesitate to ask for help and advice from your elders or other family members who have been successful!

Take Away Lessons from Chapter 3:

✓ Don't be afraid to add value above and beyond what you think the other person is expecting.

✓ Sometimes your biggest givers come from unlikely places.

Your success as a connector depends on giving value first and planting profitable seeds.

<u>NOTES</u>

Chapter 4

*Your Blueprint
to Connecting*

"FIVE YEARS FROM NOW YOU
WILL BE PRETTY MUCH THE
SAME AS YOU ARE TODAY
EXCEPT FOR TWO THINGS:
THE BOOKS YOU READ
AND THE PEOPLE
YOU GET CLOSE TO."

- CHARLES "TREMENDOUS" JONES

Think back to the first time you rode a bicycle. There were certain things you had to remember about your balance, control, how to brake, etc. Chances are, you still fell a time or two. But you got back up and kept going.

The same thing happened when you learned to drive a car, write your name in cursive, and read a map. You struggled but kept going until you mastered that particular skill.

Ask yourself who you have connected with so far and what it has meant to you. Think about the following:

1. What you have in common
2. What you have gained from this connection
3. What you want to continue to gain from this connection
4. What you have given to earn and keep this connection

Your Associations Determine Your Destinations

Experts say your income is in direct proportion of the five people you hang around most. Take a look at what you make

and pull your phone out and look at the five names that you call the most. Now take a second to analyze what they make. Hmmm... interesting! They are great people I'm sure, but if you want to go to the next level you have to start talking to people who are already at that level, not the ones who are trying to get there. This is so important that you get what I'm telling you right now.

I know you're a great and ambitious individual and you're ready to get to the top. I guarantee the only thing stopping you is a lack of opportunity. So if you start connecting with people who are already at that stage of life how much easier is it for you to attract the opportunity yourself.

Scientifically, if you want to get the best things out of life then having the wrong people around you will do nothing but paralyze you and push you further away from your dreams and desires. You don't realize it but its killing you.

Surround Yourself With Great People

Psychologist and psychiatrist point out that when thoughts are conveyed to your subconscious mind, impressions are made to the brain cells. As soon as your subconscious accepts an idea it immediately begins to put things in effect. This is not two minds: just two spheres of activity within one mind. Your conscious is your reasoning mind- the phase of mind that chooses your friends, home and partner in life. You make all

your decisions with your conscious mind. On the other hand your heart is kept functioning automatically and the processes of digestion, circulation and breathing are carried through by your subconscious mind. You unconsciously accept what you consciously believe... that means your associations determine your destinations. If you are constantly surrounded by people who have a weak mind and at the same time have a non-conducive environment you will unconsciously accept that and consciously attract the same kinds of things you see.

Your subconscious is like the soil which accepts anything that you put in it, whether it's good or bad. So if the people around you are constantly showering with negative thoughts and conditions unconsciously you are growing that from the inside and it will soon effect you externally.

All things that have happened to you are based on thoughts and impressions suppressed on your subconscious mind through belief. How you beat this is through the repetition of good thoughts frequently repeated which your subconscious mind accepts. When you surround yourself with people who are positive, productive and purposeful, eventually you will become that. You cannot afford to have people who are not speaking constantly to the King or Queen in you, The Millionaire in you, or whatever person is inside of you that you wish to become.

"Some people come into your life for a reason, some for a

season and some for a lifetime. Overtime you will learn the difference."

You have to release your friends and grow so you can meet your next connection. Most of your friends are good for the scrimmage of your life but now it's time to play the real game. Are you ready?

Power Connectors and Potential Powerhouses

If you are interested in taking an active approach to networking and making the best use of your time networking, you should identify those people in your network with whom you are the most connected with and those with whom you are the least. We will separate them into two distinct categories; those who are *Capstones* and those who are *Base Builders*.

Power Connectors

There is a relatively practical way to identify your power connectors. Write down the names of 40 people you know. These should be friends, acquaintances and colleagues but not blood relatives. Then for each of these people, determine who introduced you to that person... and who introduced you to that person... and who introduced you to that person.

As you do this for your 40 friends, acquaintances and colleagues, a pattern will begin to emerge. In fact, this is how you graphically map out your network. These exercises will reveal that what you term as your social circle is really

just a pyramid, which is to say that a large percentage of your contact originated from a relatively few number of individuals. Those individuals at the tops of these pyramids, who are known as the Capstones, are your power connectors (Connectionaires).

If you are looking to make the most of your networking efforts, focus your time and energy on any or all of your Capstones. Take them to lunch, breakfast, and coffee; give them great referrals and ideas. Find ways to add value to their business and they will do more of the same in the future for you.

Potential Powerhouses

In most fields when you find a person or company that is absolutely magnificent in their performance, they become known as a power house. Well, the world of connecting is no different. Your main goal is to become a *Connection Powerhouse.* This has dual benefits. When you fit the bill of a Connection Powerhouse, you can get more accomplished because a powerhouse is someone who has made it a point to not only connect with people but build relationships overtime into more than business connections, but to the point of friendship. He is well respected in more than just his local state but worldwide and has made a difference over time sowing into the lives of others. He's that person that everyone

knows, loves and respects because he has always been a man of his word.

When you become a Connection Powerhouse, you are more likely to attract others of the same or greater caliber, allowing you access to a vast world of unimaginable resource. However, you don't want to neglect the development of your second and third tier relationships as well. While a Connection Powerhouse is a great networking resource, there is also power in relationships that are not close at all.

In his 1974 book **Getting a Job**, sociologist Mark Granovetter indicated that through his research he found that 56 percent of people found jobs through personal contacts. This is not surprising because most of the best jobs are never officially posted.

The surprise in his research, however, was that the personal contacts used to obtain these jobs were generally not from family or close friends. The most effective contacts were those Granovetter referred to as "weak ties", or what I would prefer to refer to as *Base Builders.* According to Granovetter, of the individuals who reported that they found a job through personal contacts, 55.6 percent said that they saw their contact only occasionally and 27.8 percent indicated they saw their contact only rarely.

Therefore, when it comes to finding out about new jobs – or

for that matter, most anything related to networking – your Base Builders tend to be more important than your power connectors. This happens because your close ties tend to occupy the same world as you do. Your family, friends, co-workers and fellow entrepreneurial buddies know many of the same people you do.

On the other hand, mere acquaintances are much more likely to know something that you do not. Thus, some of the most important people in your life are those who are not close to you. In fact, to a degree, the more people you know who are not close to you, the stronger your position becomes.

If you want to build your network, have lunch with that person with whom you are only somewhat acquainted. While this effort may take you out of your comfort zone, it will lead you to much more rich relationships. The true Connectionaire knows that a breakthrough is only a connection away. And you can never tell exactly where that connection is going to come from. So keep your Capstones and your Base Builders close! Never forget the theory of the Six degrees of separation. You are only six people away from your goal, so take that extra step and reach out to that extra person, you never know where it could lead.

Power Connectors - Action steps

1. Stay connected: Write an email, send a text or call at least once every two weeks to remain fresh in the minds of your connections and continue to build the know, the like and the trust.

2. Solve Problems: Find out what their biggest need is and start working to help them fill it. This will make you much more valuable than the person who is just calling to take them to lunch and pick their brain.

3. Make it Personal: There is nothing more powerful than sending a meaningful note that expresses your appreciation for everything someone has done. Send a card or personal gift in the mail. Make it personable and they will not forget you.

It's not who you know, it's who knows you.
There is no doubt about the importance and effectiveness of networking in your career search. Networking, both online and in person, provides you the opportunity to present yourself and your career objective in a much more personal way.

Networking is essentially active, personal branding. It can also be defined as the process of identifying the unique and differentiating values that you can bring to an organization,

team and/or project. The key is communicating in a professionally memorable and consistent manner in all of your actions and outputs, both online and offline, to all current and prospective stakeholders in your career.

Many experts have said that when it comes to job search networking, *"It's not what you know, it's who you know."* However, I couldn't disagree more.

First of all, **what you know is part of the value that you bring to the table** (a.k.a. your personal brand) and therefore, it is of the utmost importance in your networking efforts.

Second and more importantly, **it's not who you know, it's who knows you**, or better yet, who knows your personal brand enough to reach out to you with an opportunity where they know you and your brand would contribute the most value.

You may know a lot of influential people, but do they think of you when an opportunity arises? No matter how outstanding a candidate you may be, networking really comes down to getting your personal brand out there in front of your career stakeholders and **communicating what you have to offer** in a memorable and consistent manner.

Leverage Facebook, LinkedIn and your email Rolodex to keep in contact with classmates, colleagues and other contacts

from your past. They have obviously seen you "in action" at various points in your life and career and may identify you for opportunities if you stay on their radar.

You Cannot Connect Alone

Search for professionals in your target companies, industries or functional areas using LinkedIn and other networks and reach out to schedule informational interviews. These are great ways to make more personal connections with potential career stakeholders and provide you relevant contacts with whom to keep in touch.

Participate in relevant online forums, as well as in LinkedIn Groups and LinkedIn Answers. This will not only help you establish your expertise and personal brand in front of other target professionals, but it also allows you to network and develop rewarding relationships.

Attend various events hosted by your professional organizations, your school, your alumni association, your church, etc. in order to physically interact with potential career contacts. Make sure to get your contacts' business cards or information so you can follow up with them in the future.

There are many more ways you can get your personal brand out there in front of others from introducing yourself to your neighbors to talking to someone sitting next to you on the subway or on a plane.

In the end, networking really falls on how well you have branded yourself to those whom you have identified as potential stakeholders in your career.

Potential Connectionaires – Action Steps

1. Stay connected: Endeavor to stay connected with the weak ties with emails or newsletters. You never know if they have a consulting gig or business opportunity that is perfect for you.

2. Reply to E-mail: No matter how many e-mails you receive each day, you can still reply to your weak ties with brief responses. If you are pressed for time then keep it to one sentence or write to tell them you will respond later.

3. Be strategic but thoughtful: **Strategic you** - Go

through your network and pick out two or three connections that you may not know that well but would like to know better. **Thoughtful you** - Pick out an article online or send them a friendly note. This will show tem that you take the time to think about them and are open to building a stronger connection.

Make a list of four people you would like to connect with.

_____

_____

_____

_____

1. **What you want from this connection**
2. **What you may have in common**
3. **How you intend to make the connection**
4. **What you have to give (your value) to earn this connection, and keep it**

Here are some more useful steps to follow as a beginner.

Step 1 - Know Your Surroundings

As a beginner, one of the first things you want to do is look at the models of the most successful people around you. Really study those people. What makes them get out of bed in the morning? What obstacles did they overcome to gain their successes?

Of course, if you don't know people personally around you that are successful, study people on TV that you may want to emulate. For example, when you look at people like Oprah, President Obama, or NBA star LeBron James, evaluate what steps you think they had to take to get to reach the level of success they have achieved. Why are these people, the best of the best? Make connections with the traits they have in common such as work ethic, education, or other personal development.

Step 2 – Start Reading!

Start reading books and listening to books on CD! One of the key reasons I am as optimistic as I am, is because of the many books I've read. I didn't have a lot of mentors growing up. So my mentors became Robert Kiyosaki, Tony Robbins, Steven Covey, and Jeffrey Gittomer.

What are you going to read? Start out reading books like the art of relationship building, how to connect or just read different blogs. Why not? Most of them are FREE!
You're already headed in the right direction if you're holding this book. This book is going to be a great resource for you.
I didn't have any extraordinary riches. It was only one year ago that I realized the potential that existed simply through the connections I already had. In fact, my connections are what inspired me to write this book, so that this book can also

help you to realize your potential in connecting and building relationships. But it all starts with doing your homework.

One of the best quotes I've heard is from author Jim Rohn, "If you want to be rich, study rich people. If you want to be smart, study smart people."

If you want to be good at building relationships, study books about people who build relationships or look at people that

have great relationships. President Obama is a person that
has built great relationships. Just think, four years ago he was
relatively unknown. Since then, he has become the leader of
the free world.

Step 3 – Prepare Your Introduction!

Eventually you'll want to go to different networking and
connecting events. Before you go to a place where you'll meet
people, you'll need to be prepared with a KILLER 30 second
introduction.

 You'll notice I didn't call them "elevator speeches", which
they are often and popularly termed. The idea there is that you
are trapped in an elevator with the connection of your dreams
and they have no choice but to listen to you for 30 seconds,
giving you your opportunity to pitch your finest! I am more
prone to believe that in such a scenario, your potential
connection would be more anxious to get out of the elevator
and less likely to pay any attention to what you are saying, no
matter how good it could be. What's worse is that they will
reference you from that point on by the unpleasant experience
in the elevator and make it a point to get away from you!
Besides, how many people really give elevator speeches... I
never have! ☺

The Reason why I say you should have a 30 second Super
Commercial is because the whole point of telling a potential

connection what you do is to ***engage*** them, and what engages more people in the United States in 30 Seconds besides Super Bowl commercials. I specify Super Bowl because some commercials engage you and others make you get the remote and TiVo to the next commercial. The Super Bowl is often the platform for the most creative and ground breaking commercials ever to hit the screen. For those of you that don't know what the Super Bowl is let me give you some brief history.

The first Sunday in February is always Super Bowl Sunday.

The price tag for a 30-second ad slot also follows tradition: averaging $2.7 to $3 million in 2008.

According to Wikipedia, the Super Bowl, the championship game of the National Football League in the United States, is known for the high-profile advertisements that air during its television broadcast. The broadcast typically ranks very highly in the Nielsen ratings, reaching more than 90 million viewers. Prices for advertising space can typically cost millions of dollars; 30 seconds of advertising time during the 2010 telecast is expected to cost US $3.01 million.

"There is no other way in the U.S. to reach the amount of people that you can with the Super Bowl", says Richard Castellini, chief marketing officer of job search site CareerBuilder.com. The high price tags of the commercials

all but promises that they will be spectacular and innovative in most cases. The commercials are often highly anticipated, generating much buzz even before the game is played usually because of their innovation or sense of humor.

You should look at every connection as the time in between the Super Bowl. Every networking opportunity is the main event and you have to put out the best advertisement in order to sale your product. Treat is as if you paid 3 million dollars for this opportunity. If you're anything like me, I'm sure you don't have that kind of money to waste, so prepare in advance. There are two directions to take when crafting your Super Bowl Commercial. Remember you can choose any commercial that you want!

THE "HIGH DEF" COMMERCIAL: This one's easy if you're just meeting someone for the first time. Take the pressure off of yourself by asking the individual about their current business. Actually ASK about their business. In fact, I usually word it best this way, "Because of the amount of time I spend speaking and travelling, I've become an expert in putting together people who can make money from each other. Tell me a little bit about what you do and I'll go through my list of contacts mentally and see if there isn't someone that would be a great customer for you!"

THE "WHAT DO YOU DO?" COMMERCIAL: Who

hasn't heard this one? "So – what do you do?" This is where your Superbowl Commercial will shine! Now's your chance to take out your business card, hand it to them, and give a 30 second talk on just how much you can help THEM! Be careful not to glorify yourself too much though, make sure your pitch is focused on the other party. Write out your commercial and count how many times the word "I" appears in it. More than once and you're probably just talking about yourself!

My Commercial - My Name is Rob Coats and I'm President of Connect Your Life, Author of Connect and Grow Rich and Affectionately called "The Connectionaire." I bring Sexy to the word Networking and I make Connecting Look Damn Easy! I turn acquaintances into friends and contacts into contracts. Over the last 6 years I've helped over 2,000 people find the right opportunities and that's turned into just over 20 million dollars in new business. What is it that you do?

If you remember that people are always more interested in how you can help them, you're on the right track. Keep that in the top of your mind when composing your speech.

Here's a few more examples to improve the two examples mentioned above:

I know an Avon representative who says: "I help women look beautiful."

Or a business coach that says: "I help you get more clients than you know what to do with."

And here's my favorite, one that is used by an IRS agent: "I'm a government fund-raiser."

Once you've created your 30 Second Super Bowl Commercial, practice it regularly so that it flows smoothly. When reciting your pitch convey passion, confidence, and instill some of your personality into it. Believe me it makes a *HUGE* difference when you add feeling to it.

Remember:

Shut Up! - Once you have said what you came to say, stop talking. You will have said enough for your connection to ask you directly for more information in a one on one interaction.

Stand Out: Tell them something that they have never heard of. I don't care if it's ridiculous if that's going to have them wanting to hear more. You'd be surprised that what you think is corny may actually end up being liked by the other person because you chose to be different.

Passion: Convey passion, confidence, and instill some of your personality into the pitch.

It's about THEM not YOU. By now you should know people are more concerned about themselves and everyone else

comes second. If you are in a profession they hear from often, they will be familiar with the general message and filter it out.

Step 4 – Just Do It

Just get out there and do it. Don't take too much time. Don't feel like you have to be an expert at connecting before you start doing it. You're going to make mistakes. That's how you learn. As long as you ***fail forward*** and don't go backwards, you'll ultimately win.

- **Maintain your contacts**

- **Write 5 compelling emails a day.**

- **Write them twice a month.**

- **Help or Volunteer to be of service to them.**

A Final Crucial Step – Get a Mentor!

The other key is having a mentor. This is a person that can help to guide you and give you encouragement as you grow and develop into the connectionaire you will become! I take pride in mentoring others to make their journey that much easier and beneficial.

Find out how you can have the Connectionaire™, Rob Coats, as your personal mentor at www.Connectionaire.com!

Even if you don't choose me, I would still recommend that
you get a mentor or a coach to help you if for no other reason
than to shorten your learning curve. That's what mentors do!
They can assist you by sharing with you the mistakes they
made in the past so you don't have to make them now or in
the future.

What's your name again?

In order to be a successful connectionaire, you have to
become a pro at learning and remembering names.
How many times have you been out, ran into a familiar face,
started talking to the person and they say "you don't even
remember my name." On top of that, you feel guilty because
they not only remember your name but they also remember
what you do, how many kids you have and your favorite
movie! It can be pretty embarrassing.
Over the years, I've learned a couple of techniques to help
develop this skill. The first is the association of a famous
name with a person to remember their names. For example,
if you meet someone named Britney Smith, think of the
most famous person you know with a similar name. My first
thought is Britney Spears. Every time you see her you'll
associate Britney Spears' face with her name, allowing you to
remember it!
The second method is associating a name with a VISUAL
image. When coming up with the image, there is one

important rule to remember: **it must be ridiculous and illogical** – it should NOT make sense. Why? Because if it does, then it's boring and therefore, **NOT** memorable. You make it ridiculous by employing these methods: exaggerated size and/or numbers and animation (it should be moving). The more ridiculous it is, the more memorable.

Example: You meet a person named Marley who has dread-locked hair – I've just visualized a super-sized Reggae band standing behind him playing Bob Marley's "I Shot the Sheriff"–chances are, you'll remember the person and his name for a long while.

Tools of the Trade

Now that you have what you need to get started, you're probably wondering what tools you'll need to help you along the way.

One of the most vital tools you can have is business cards. Business cards are NOT that expensive. Even if you don't know your title, or you don't have a job, put on there what you *envision* yourself being. Just remember you don't have to wait for your business cards to arrive in order to start connecting!

Get your business cards, get a website, and do something to get people talking about you!

If you could only choose one medium to use to brand yourself, then brand yourself online. If you don't know how

to brand yourself on Facebook or other social networks, there are millions of blogs out there that can teach you how to do it; even books at your local bookstore!

FYI: check out Peter Montoya's book ***The Brand Called You***. It's a great read.

If you don't have a computer, go to the library. It's free. But start compiling your profile online. Many people say, "Oh, I don't want people getting my information." That attitude should be the first thing out the door. The point of connecting is to meet the maximum number of people necessary to help you accomplish your goals and also to build new relationships. Plus, if The President of the United States of America is on LinkedIn, why aren't you?

Try visiting www.Media.com, and put in whatever you're searching to do. If you want to do networking that's strictly and mainly for IT professionals, then that's what your search criteria would be. It helps you focus your search and get useful information instead of blind searching and ending up with a lot of unnecessary information.

If you want to be an entrepreneur, you can go to www. networkinglifenow.com and learn what it takes to go out on your own.

You can also join Facebook, Twitter, or LinkedIn for free to help establish your presence in the world of social media. Lastly, visit www.Connectionaire.com and sign up for our members-only group and meet like-minded connection-

makers like yourself!

You have the world at your fingertips right now. There are so many experts and books out there already written on what you want to do. You just have to be willing to go and search for the information you need.

Make Your Perception People's Reality

In college I dressed up almost every day. You ask why? I just liked the way I felt. I lived by the motto, "when you look good you feel good." Students and professors alike treated me differently. I had a sort of successful swag about myself and because I believed it, unconsciously, I made others believe it. And this was at a point when I didn't have any real money. My advice is to always put your best foot forward and dress to impress.

Most of you all have heard the saying "You have to fake it 'til you make it!"

Well it is absolutely true! There are going to be times in your life where you are not doing as well as you should be doing (i.e. you're broke), and people will be waiting to discredit you. I know everybody wants you to believe in the "we are the world" song and everything is peas and carrots but the truth is, people can't wait to hate on you. They'll look to attack you especially if you were successful at one point. As another saying goes, misery loves company.

There will be times when it will be difficult to be transparent.

More often than people want to know about your struggles, they want to know about your successes. In business, it is important that your customers and clients have confidence in who you are, and by presenting a clean and professional image, you provide them with that peace of mind. Just remember that when you are "faking" it, you're not being deceitful, you're simply showing the world who you will become!

In addition, you should know that perception is just that... perception. Be conscious not to take people at "face value". Connect with everyone as if they are the one person that may take you to the next level, because they just might be!

Take Away Lessons from Chapter 4:

✓ Remember the key steps to getting started: Know Your Surroundings, Start Reading, Prepare Your Introduction and Just Do It!

✓ Get a mentor like the Connectionaire™ to take years off your learning curve and ease your transition into becoming a successful connector!

✓ Don't forget your tools: Get business cards, make your presence known online and get people talking about you!

✓ Take advantage of free social networking sites to start connecting immediately!

✓ UP YOURS! Image of Course. Present the world with the best version of yourself.

✓ Remember: Just because people judge you by your appearance "DOES NOT" mean you should do the same.

✓ Give everyone a fair shot while you are connecting and growing rich.

✓ For more info on upping your image check www.connectionaire.com

<u>NOTES</u>

Chapter 5

Listen With Your Eyes

"I SPEAK TWO LANGUAGES,
BODY AND ENGLISH."

- MAE WEST

Of all the many and various forms of self expression, Body Language is the highest from of communication. Albert Mehialian, pioneer researcher of body language in the 1950's, found that the total impact of a message is about 7 percent verbal (words only) and 38 percent vocal (including tone fo voice, inflection and other sounds) and 55 percent nonverbal.

If you want to connect with someone, would you agree that you both need to make sure you speak the right language? The importance of that non-verbal connection is exactly why I'm going to show you the power of recognizing body language.

First off, whether you know it or not, what people say is not always what they really mean or feel. As we've learned before, people can become protective of their own feelings and often times will be very elusive of the true nature of their desires.

Growing up my house was the hangout hub for me and all

of my friends. At any given point in the day, there would be kids playing on video systems, playing basketball in the front yard or posted up in the kitchen, eating all the food in the refrigerator. When everyone had left for the day my mom would often say to me, "I don't want Ramone coming back to this house, I don't trust him." Ramone was a friend of mine that wasn't as "fortunate" as we were (even though we weren't living too high on the hog either), and despite his unseemly disposition, I enjoyed having him as a friend. Hearing my mother say this in turn would irritate me because she had never even spoken to him. How could she say that about him? He's a good guy.

Two days later I would know that she was right and I should have listened because my new Jordan's had come up missing, and all of sudden Ramone, who usually sported the beat up Sikes (fake Nike's), had on the identical pair of shoes... same size and all.

So what I realized when I started studying body language was that my mother, and for that matter, women in general are far more intuitive and able to read body language then men. I guess that's why they say trust a woman's intuition. According to the Definitive Book of Body Language by Allen and Barbara Pease "women have an innate ability to pick up and decipher nonverbal signals, as well as having an accurate eye for small details." This is another reason why Mother's

always know when we are lying! All this time I thought they were just psychic!

However, this is not a skill that is indigenous to those of the female persuasion. While women can read people subconsciously, anyone can teach themselves consciously to read the signals.

The rules for Reading People

What you see and hear in any situation does not necessarily reflect the real attitudes people may actually have. According to The Definite Book of Body Language there are three basic rules to get things right.

Rule 2: Look for Congruence

One of the most serious errors beginners make in learning body language is to interpret a solitary gesture in isolation of other gestures or circumstances. Isolated, a gesture can be simply a coincidence, but combined with a series of gestures, that single gesture becomes a clue to solving a puzzle.

Gestures come in sentences called "clusters" and invariably reveal the truth about a person's feeling or attitudes. A body language cluster is like a verbal sentence, it needs at least three words in it before you can accurately define each of the words.

Ex: Scratching the head can mean uncertainty, but it's also a sign of dandruff. So always look for at least 3 things before making a judgement.

Rule 1: Read Gestures in Clusters:

Research shows that nonverbal signals carry about five times as much impact as the verbal channel and that, when the two are incongruent, people--especially women-- rely on the nonverbal message and disregard the verbal content.

"When a person's words and body language are in conflict, women ignore what is said."

Sigmund Freud once reported that while a patient was verbally expressing happiness with her marriage, she was unconsciously slipping her wedding ring on and off her finger. Freud was aware of the significance of this unconscious gesture and was not surprised when marriage problems began to surface.

Rule 3: Read Gestures in Context

You have to read body language in the context in which they occur. For example if freezing outside and someone has their arms and legs crossed tightly and their chin down it doesn't mean they're mad...they're just cold. If, however, you are trying to approach someone of the opposite sex and as you are talking they perform the same cluster of gestures, and the

weather is great... Chances are you might as well not waste your time.

Can You Fake It?

I know a lot of you are asking can you fake body language. The general answer is no, because of the lack of congruence that is likely to occur between the main gestures, micro signals, and the spoken words. For example, open palms are associated with honesty, but when the faker holds his hands out and smiles at you and he tells a lie, his micro gestures give him away. His pupils may contract, one eyebrow may lift, or the corner of his mouth may twitch, and these signals contradict the Open Palm gesture and sincere smile. The result is that the receivers especially women, tend not to believe what they hear.

"Body language is easier to fake with men than with women because, overall, men aren't good readers of body language."

How to Become A Beasty (Great) Reader

Set aside at least 15 minutes a day to study the body language of other people, as well as acquiring a conscious awareness of your own gestures. A good reading ground is anywhere that people meet and interact. Social functions, business meetings, parties, airports or church are good places to observe the entire spectrum of human gestures.

Learning to read body language signals not only makes you more accurately aware of others trying to dominate and manipulate, it brings the realization that others are also doing the same to us and, most important, it teaches us to be more sensitive to other people's feelings and emotions. It is also said that only 7% of professionals use these skills and on average they make over $250,000 annually.

Take away Lessons for Chapter 5

- Recognize that people communicate on many levels. Watch their facial expressions, eye contact, posture, hand and feet movements, body movement and placement, and appearance and passage as they walk toward you. Every gesture is communicating something if you listen with your eyes. Become accustomed to watching nonverbal communication and your ability to read nonverbal communication will grow with practice.

- Face- Look like you care. Eye contact builds rapport. Don't use fake smiles.

- Your body- Gestures are a natural extension of your feelings. Stand with your feet shoulder width apart. Don't look off while the other person is talking. Give a firm handshake

- If a person's words say one thing and their body language says another, listen to the nonverbal communication –that is usually the correct decision.

- When connecting with someone, whether at a social or networking event, recognize that nonverbal cues can tell you:

  --when you've talked long enough,

--when someone else wants to speak, and

--the mood of the person and their reaction to your remarks.

Listen to them and you'll be a better connect.

Understanding nonverbal communication improves with practice. The first step in practice is to recognize the power of nonverbal communication. I'm sure you've had gut feelings that what a person said to you was untrue. Listen to your gut. Along with your life experiences, training, beliefs and all that make up your past, it's your inner expert on nonverbal communication.

<u>NOTES</u>

Chapter 6

The Power of Connecting

"WHAT LIES BEHIND YOU AND WHAT LIES IN FRONT OF YOU, PALES IN COMPARISON TO WHAT LIES INSIDE OF YOU."

- RALPH WALDO EMERSON

In the world of connecting, there are going to be success
stories, and…there are going to be horror stories. They say
a man should learn from the past failures and successes of
others. Here are just a few personal experiences I've had
over the years. As you read them, I hope you can use these
experiences to fuel your own connections!

Connections Within Arms Reach

Awhile back I was dating a young lady by the name of Pam
who is the editor of a magazine. Being as how she was
directly associated with a popular news outlet, she was able
to connect regularly with influential people. This was always
impressive but it became extremely useful to me when my
mom was diagnosed with breast cancer. A friend of Pam's
had interviewed a woman named Mary Jenkins, who is the
founder and president of an organization called Christians
Overcoming Cancer (COC). The organization helps cancer
patients with their bills and other needs while they battle the
disease.

Pam gave my mother the contact information for COC and my mother called on the day of her first chemotherapy appointment. She was nervous and scared but she was able to connect directly with Mary Jenkins. She told my mother, "I want to be there for your experience," and proceeded to travel nearly 2 hours to be there with her. Ms Jenkins arrived in time to be with my mother right before her first treatment, and she then stayed for the duration of the appointment encouraging her and giving her words of wisdom.

See Ms Jenkins knew firsthand the pain my mother would be going though having been a cancer survivor herself. Through her own compassion and selflessness, she was able to give my mother the friend and confidant she needed at the exact moment she needed it. My mother is now a lifelong friend to her and would do anything she could to help her.

So through a three tier connection process, I was able to connect my mother with Ms. Mary Jenkins, the very person that would be able to help her on various projects and with certain bills, all within the first hour of my mother calling Christians Overcoming Cancer.

Whether she knew it or not at the time, Mary was being a Connectionaire! She was genuine when she connected with my family, she is a loving, caring and encouraging person, and she also sought to *add value first*, never asking for anything in return. As a result of her helping my mother, I've raised thousands of dollars for COC through my Network

Your Life events. She didn't have to she supported my mother and I wanted to support her program, but even if she had never given my mother a dime, I still would have tried to help because of who she is as a person.

To find out how you can donate to Christians Overcoming Cancer, visit them online at www. ChristiansOvercomingCancer.com

Who Are You Calling A Loser?

A friend of mine, Rachel Young, had a great website teaching people how to lose weight. She had lost 80 pounds herself, and wanted to share her successes and failures with other people battling with weight loss, or the lack thereof (www. WhatIfYouWereThin). People always asked her about her weight loss, as if she'd received some "secret memo" or key to unlock the door to getting rid of fat that the rest of the world never got. It occurred to her that other people who've lost a great amount of weight face the same issue. People who have been on national television would be inundated with get-thin-quick seekers.

Rachel began using the power of Facebook to start reaching out to former contestants from the NBC show "The Biggest Loser" and found them to be very receptive to her emails. She asked them about things other than the show in order to build rapport and prevent it from sounding like another

TV interview. Before long, she'd interviewed most of the winners from the show and was creating a book based on her conversations with the reality show stars. She wanted them to talk about their lives and their struggles, and even prompted them to talk about books they have coming out to promote themselves rather than the show.

This allowed Rachel to add pertinent information from popular and reliable sources to her book as well as her website. This transaction was mutually beneficial between Rachel and the newly budding stars as they were now offered an additional outlet for their own personal progress as well as access to potential fans and resources.

A little time and know-how allowed her to create a book from thin air…all because she used the power of Facebook to make the connection– and it cost her nothing financially!!

"When you lose, don't lose the lesson."
– The Dalai Lama

You Might Not Get It Right…

About three years ago, my ex-girlfriend's father owned a dry cleaning business located in a plaza with several other stores. The owner of the neighboring shoe store approached my girlfriend's father, Tom, and said, "You know, I'm really

impressed with you and may have an opportunity for you. I have 99 stores all across the country. My cash flow is millions of dollars a month. But, I'm about ready to get out of it and move back to India." He offered Tom the opportunity to either take over the existing store, or purchase one of the other 99 stores nationwide.

Tom, his daughter (my girlfriend), me, and another friend decided to take a chance and get in on the deal. We began by spending time at the shoe store, building the relationship and learning about the trade. The guy seems really cool. He invites us to come down and says he'll even show us how to run the store. He gives us valuable tidbits such as; "We're getting the shoes from China for this amount, we sell them for this amount." He gives us the necessary books and even invites us to stay in his house on occasion! It still seems like a dream at this time but we're thinking, "This guy truly wants us to succeed, this is such a wonderful opportunity."

We lay out a set of goals for ourselves with 2 main tasks: 1 – to find the right location, and 2 – to secure the startup fee of $30,000. It takes us a couple of months of searching and we finally find a great location. Our research is impeccable and we put together a simple, 25 page business plan. Between the four of us, we proffer the necessary startup money, so now we're ready!

Tom calls the shoe store owner. No answer. A week goes by,

and another. 2 whole weeks and still no answer, of course by this time we're fuming. Months of work have gone down the drain as quick as the opportunity had came.

Finally, my girlfriend went to the shop and got some results. She discovered that the man we'd been working with wasn't there, and in fact, there was a *new* guy there. The other guy had been fired. It turns out that the store was owned corporately. All 99 stores were actually a large chain owned by a larger company. And to add insult to injury; the final nail in the coffin - to run a store like this isn't $30,000... the startup is more like $100,000.

If that wasn't enough, while putting our plan together and collecting the resources we needed, we'd showed our business plan to a company who said they'd help us with the funding we were looking for. Guess who got the lease on the property we were attempting to buy? You guessed it – we were stabbed in the back. In fact, their store is still operating in that same location to this day. But we don't want to give up. We resolve simply to change gears, reasoning that as long as we don't stop, we'll still come out successful.

A Lesson Learned

Now, some of you might say the lesson here is that you can't trust everybody that you come in contact with. The worst mistake you could make here is ignoring the lesson. As I said

at the beginning of this chapter, not every connection will turn out the way you expect it to. The best thing you can do is to learn from the mistakes, errors, or mishaps that come your way.

The REAL lesson is that we didn't quit. We chose to look at the positive. Even though we were taken by surprise, we didn't stop trying. We didn't stop learning. We realized that we still had a functioning business plan, 4 intelligent partners, and $30,000 of investment money. We kept going and eventually found a place to invest our money that we'd done the research on ahead of time and felt confident in.

At the end of the day, the only way we knew 100% that we'd fail is if we were to stop trying altogether, and that's what separates those who continue to develop and grow successful connections from those who are just looking for someone to help them one time.

Action Steps from Chapter 6:

- Are you already connected with someone on a social networking site that could help you grow your business? Many celebrities, authors, and sports stars have profiles online that allow you to become "friends" with them. Using your list of people you WANT to be connected with from Chapter 1, find these stars on Twitter, Facebook, or LinkedIn and start connecting with them. Remember WIIFM! Establish a relationship first, then you can move on to business growth.

- You'll notice the connection success stories in this chapter outweigh the horror stories. Don't be afraid to make a connectionship with someone who could benefit you. Rachel Young says, "Prosperity favors the prepared." Don't wait until tomorrow to start making your connections online! The web is open 24/7!

Take Away Lessons from Chapter 6:

- ✓ You never know how close you are to meeting the person want to see until you ask the people you know.

- ✓ Don't ever quit. You could be just one step away from the biggest success of your life!

- ✓ Establish the relationship first. Period.

- ✓ Remember the Dalai Lama's words, "When you lose, don't lose the lesson."

<u>NOTES</u>

Chapter 7

Maximizing Your Connections

"THE BIGGER PROBLEMS
THAT YOU SOLVE, THE
BIGGER PAYCHECK YOU WILL
RECEIVE."

- (AUTHOR UNKNOWN)

So now let's address the question that I know has been looming in your mind; can making connections actually make you money? The short answer is – *yes*! You can have the benefits of money and so much more! There's more to building a successful "power network" than merely making money.

I've made money and sometimes better than money. One of the other advantages of connecting can come in the form of "freebies." NFL games, NBA games, concerts, and trips to different countries. I've gotten them all for free. I've enjoyed all of these opportunities simply because of the connections I've made. I've lived my life like a rock star without actually being a rock star.

One of the keys to making money from connections is through helping a person – the more influential the person you help solve a problem, the more you'll benefit from that relationship; tangibly and intangibly.

According to Brian Uzzi and Shannon Dunlap, in their

Harvard Business Article on How to Build Your Network, two keys or advantages to developing networks and establishing relationships that I want to touch on:

1. **Private Information**

2. **Access to Diverse Skill Sets**

Private Information

Private information is key in most business transactions. And when I say private information, I'm not talking about "insider trading". I'm talking about advanced notice of release dates for a new product or book. I'm talking about knowing the boss' favorite color because you have lunch with his assistant. Or maybe you know the specific characteristics a particular company looks for in its job applicants all because you have access to private information.

Keep in mind that a lot of this information is "relative" – meaning that what may seem important to you may not be as important to someone else. The important coherent to having private information is knowing how to apply it.

The Pizza Guy Delivers!

The real estate investing arena is highly competitive. Many investors are constantly looking to get the upper hand

whenever and however possible. A friend of mine in Atlanta was no exception. At the time this story took place, the average homeowner facing foreclosure in the Atlanta market could expect to receive over 100 letters a day from investors, real estate professionals, and mortgage lenders.

Needless to say, my friend was treading water. He was using the same public information that everyone else had access to, and as a result, he was showing up to the party at the same time as everyone else.

One day, my friend ordered a pizza, nothing special, just an ordinary day, it didn't seem like a big deal at the time. When the driver delivered the pizza, my friend paid with his credit card... the card that had his business name on it.

A brief conversation with the driver about the real estate industry and local available property gave my friend the inside information he'd been looking for! As it turned out, the driver often knew when a home was going on the market before the sign went up in the front yard. He had the rare privilege of catching a glimpse inside the houses of people who were packing as he delivered the pizza to their house – and what do people NOT want to do when they're packing to move? Cook.

Seeing the advantage and opportunity, my friend acted quickly, offering to pay a "finder's fee" to the pizza delivery driver for information about local property that was going on

the market – BEFORE anyone else knew about it.

He was able to use private information to gain access to these homeowners before his competition could... and he made over 7 figures that year as a result! All because he ordered a large pepperoni!

Diverse Skill Sets

Have you ever been inspired by something that had absolutely NOTHING to do with what you were inspired to do?

The sound of a diesel engine may inspire a car enthusiast to create better insulation for homes (the earlier model of the

diesel engine was very loud and noisy), which may inspire someone else to use a specific color for their company colors and you may wind up with the Pink Panther as your company mascot.

The point is that the people you network with can bring a variety of knowledge and information to the table. It's like a Thanksgiving buffet of information and your best bet is to diversify the menu! As a connectionaire, you're free to pick and choose the information you deem the most worthy to what you aspire to do, be, or create, and apply it as you see fit.

Example Story – From Injured Player to LinkedIn Superstar

In the spring of 2007, after a highly successful career in high school and college football, Lewis Howes earned a spot on an arena football team. During the second game of the season, he dove to catch the football and unfortunately slammed into the playing surface severely breaking his wrist.

Even though he finished the season with his hand taped, at the end of the season he took the team doctor's advice and had surgery. The surgery turned out to be more complicated than anyone imagined. The doctors had to take a piece of bone from his hip and fuse it to his wrist bone.

What was only supposed to be a few weeks in a cast turned into six months, which lead to depression and a lack of

focus and motivation. The full cast was preventing him from working so he decided to complete his undergraduate degree at Capital University in Columbus Ohio. In addition, he worked on various aspects of personal development. This included developing his leadership skills, becoming a professional speaker and being more proficient with the internet.

Example Story –
From Injured to LinkedIn Superstar

In late Fall 2007, he vowed to immerse himself in learning how to utilize the internet more effectively. He started tinkering with LinkedIn and in February 2008, he created a professional athlete network. Today, his group is the largest network of professional athletes on LinkedIn, which has over 40 million users. He is now a LinkedIn Superstar and is quickly becoming one the leading internet marketers on the World Wide Web.

Lewis Howes is proof that there is no such thing as a setback. Every fall or failure can be looked at as an opportunity to improve yourself. Sometimes you will have the opportunity to reach success on the same things that you failed at, but often times an unexpected turn can lead to a new path and an opportunity to flourish elsewhere. The Power you will have access to as a Connectionaire will astound you, amaze you, and open doors you didn't even know existed!

> ## *"It's not who you know, it's who knows you!"*
> ## *– Jeffrey Gitomer*

8 Powerful Conversation Starters

I was recently cutting the hair of a friend who is a sophomore in college at Ohio State University and he was very troubled about networking. Now here's a guy that had made over $100k at the age of 16 by doing computer consulting for companies, so by no means does he lack intelligence. His challenge, however, was his social skills. He told me that he didn't feel like he had interpersonal skills because he was either on the computer 8 hours a day, or studying for the 23 credit hours that he was taking this semester. He told me he found it hard to keep conversations going past the point of: "Hi my name is ____ and I'm a student at Ohio State".

His dilemma is very common for most people in society today but is very simple to master. If you want to become effective with communication just master the art of **asking the right questions**.

The best opening questions are those that encourage people to speak about themselves, or their work, passions, family, or experiences. Remember people love talking about themselves.

Making the conversation about them in the very beginning lets you see what kind of person they are and also can help you to find some common ground

Here are 8 great questions to open up any conversation:

- As the owner of a business, what do you find to be the two or three greatest challenges you face?

- How do you relieve the stress of your work?

- How did you get into your line of work?

- Who are your role models and how did you come to choosing them?

- When did you decide to go after your passion?

- How has your year been?

- What's the best lesson you learned from last year?

- If you could live and work anywhere, where would it be?

So with that being said, if want to know how to keep the conversation flowing, MEMORIZE these questions. Don't just glance at these and take notes but make it a conscious decision to know these like you know the back of your hand. I guarantee these will get you past the quiet awkward moments. Lastly, remember to be "Yourself." You never know if the

person on the other end has had (or is having) the very same conflicts you have!

> *"Leap and the net will appear. There will be a thousand*
> *unseen bands waiting just for you."*
> *– Joseph Campbell*

Be A Chameleon

Learn to adapt to any environment and study different people. To get what you have never gotten you must go where you have never been. Know the other, know yourself and the victory will not be a risk; know the ground, know the natural conditions, and the victory will be total. Napoleon Bonaparte was a master at taking in as much as possible with his own eyes. That's one of the reasons he was so successful when he engaged in war.

You have to learn to start looking at the people you want to connect with from their point of view. When you study an individual or group, your goal is to get inside their minds, their experiences and their way of looking at things.

Your ability to mix it up with all the right people means that you are drifting into a leadership role – that is if you aren't already filling it.

What you need to do is get maximum interaction with your connections. This is going to take you getting out of your comfort zone. You really have to have an open and fearless spirit.

Realize that to reach people you must have access to their inner lives. Give an ear to their frustration, aspiration, goals and passions. Get all of it.

Shared Experience is also a very powerful way to build your relationships with your current and new connections. When I'm feeling people out and I sense they have a good heart I will share a story that may be a little personal no matter if it's our first conversation or twentieth. I don't have a time limit, only an instinct that I feel. Seeing that I'm secure enough to be vulnerable can lead to them telling me a similar story. They might not share this story under normal circumstances, but since we both have shared experiences we have a higher level of trust. This is how you turn a contact into a connection. What used to be just an acquaintance will become a friend. Your overall goal in connecting should be turn to your connects into your friends.

"At the end of the day, people want to do business with friends"
– Jeffery Gitomer

Utilizing Social Media to Connect

George Fraser is considered by many to be the number one networking guru in the country right now.

He's built the biggest power networking conferences in the country for the last eight years. He's in the Guinness Book of World Records for organizing the biggest balloon drop. He has keys to 15 cities, three bestselling books, and is just an all around incredible, amazing person and I was able to connect with him by simply going online.

After a Network Your Life event, my keynote speaker, a celebrity shoe designer, asked why I didn't have George Fraser come speak. At the time I was unfamiliar with Mr. Fraser and so; my homework began. I researched him on the internet and finding a plethora of information, decided he would be the perfect speaker for our next event. I scoured social media sites and found him on *LinkedIn.* I sent him a message, explaining who I was and how I was inspired by his message. I did not ask him for anything, my mission was only to connect. Within 30 minutes he responded with his cell phone number. After a 10 minute conversation I was able to book him for an event with my company! It's not the first time I've connected with and booked successful speakers that way. I frequently connect with them online through social media and bring them out for fractions of the cost.

I've connected businesses together many times over and created a profit of hundreds of thousands of dollars for my time.

Extend Your Hand Without Expectations

One day, while out enjoying lunch, I bumped into an old friend. He told me one of his businesses was looking for funding for several million dollars. Though his organization was able to raise 12 million dollars through investors; when the recession hit they pulled out leaving them with only 5 million. That left them 8 million short of their goal.

Always looking to leverage my connections to help others, I started thinking. I have another friend in Los Angeles named Manny whose job is raising funds and capital. He helps businesses, different commercial companies and other similar entities get loans and secure funding. I told my funds-deficient friend that I would make some calls to see if I could help. Here's the coolest thing about connecting - I had no intention of gaining anything from this exchange! I just wanted to help my friend solve his problem. That same night, I called my friend Manny in LA explaining the situation, and I connected him with my friend.

Time passed and I was returning from a trip. My friend called me and said, "Rob, the deal is good. I mean the deal is going to be a *really* good deal. And I just want to let you know for

referring this to me, you're going to get two percent of the deal." Just last week their loan was approved. But the loan isn't for $8 million, it was actually for *$19 million*!

Who knew that a genuine, friendly gesture in a local eatery could turn into a commission of over $500,000???

I didn't have to work for that. I didn't put any time in that. I didn't put any sweat into it. And those are the results you get by giving value first. That's how you make money connecting in its purest form.

What if You Haven't Started Your Business Yet?

You may be wondering if you have to have a business right now in order to start using your relationships to make money?

Absolutely not.

On the contrary, the key is that you want to start building your network before you need it. You want to start building relationships with people before you have a business or are looking for a job. This way when you are ready to make moves toward your business or profession, you have relationships already built that can help you along the way.

There's a famous Chinese Proverb that says, "Dig the well before you are thirsty."

The faster you start learning how to connect with people, add

value, love, serve and be a blessing, the better, stronger, and more powerful your network will be.

As a beginner, you're basically building for your needs. Too many times, people wait until they need something to call someone, but by then it's too late.

I know a lady who's a grant reviewer. We were talking one day about the process of selecting a grantee. She said it's often obvious by the look and feel of the proposal if the person who put it together knew what they were doing. Another thing she did share was how big a factor it can be if you know the person's work and character whose name is on the proposal. She said when that happens, that almost automatically bumps them higher on the list in the selection process. This is simply through building rapport with that person and knowing who they are as well as the quality of their work. While many grant reviewers' names are anonymous, this bodes in your favor to build *connectionships* because you never know how this will work in your favor.

Action Steps from Chapter 7:

- Find one person that YOU can give Private Information, Access to Diverse Skill Sets, and Power to. Remember, connectionships are a two-way street!

- If you haven't already, create profiles on LinkedIn, Facebook, and other social networking sites so you can begin your online connectionships! (Don't worry, we'll go into these sites in more detail later in the book. Right now, just make the profiles!)

Take Away Lessons from Chapter 7:

✓ There are three main advantages to networking and connecting: Private Information, Access to Diverse Skill Sets, and Power.

✓ Private Information can give you access to valuable material before your competition (but it's relative, so be careful!)

✓ Accessing Diverse Skill Sets through your connections can take you farther than you ever thought possible!

✓ "Dig the well before you are thirsty"!

✓ Be prepared to make a connection and add value

wherever you are.

Use your existing connections to make new connections. "Some of the finest gemstones are found in your own backyard." – Russell Conwell

Connect & Grow *Rich*

NOTES

Chapter 8

Connection Killers

"...BEGINNING TODAY, TREAT EVERYONE YOU MEET FRIEND OR FOE, LOVED ONE OR STRANGER, AS IF THEY WERE GOING TO BE DEAD AT MIDKNIGHT. EXTEND TO EACH PERSON, NO MATTER HOW TRIVIAL THE CONTACT, ALL THE CARE AND KINDNESS AND UNDERSTANDING AND LOVETHAT YOU CAN MUSTER, AND DO IT WITH NO THOUGHT OF ANY REWARD. YOUR LIFE WILL NEVER BE THE SAME AGAIN."

- OG MANDINO

In the book **Climbing the Executive Ladder**, George Kienzle
and Edward Dave write: "Few things will pay you bigger
dividends than the time and trouble you take to understand
people." Almost nothing will add more to your stature as
a Connectionaire and as a person. Nothing will give you a
greater satisfaction or bring you more happiness. Becoming
a highly relational person can bring both individual and team
success.

A television host says to a 16 year old (at the time) Stevie
Wonder: "You have been sightless since birth. We who are
fortunate to see can sort of spend time with people and look at
them and kind of decide for ourselves if they're good people
or if we like them. How do you, being sightless, form an
opinion of someone? Stevie responds with, "Well actually,
I think my being blind helps! You see, sometimes you might
judge a person by the way they look and that's not very good.
You have to look at their personality and a blind person has to
pay very close attention to that!"

7 Connection Killers

How you perceive a person will influence how you approach
a person. Ask yourself what eyes are you looking through?
An incorrect assessment can be mean the simultaneous
beginning and ending of a potential connection. Fashion faux
pas. Freudian slips. Even the sport of baseball has errors.
Connecting is no different. You can make some very serious
relationship-ending mistakes if you aren't careful!

Let's take a look at the Top 7 Connection Killers and how to
avoid them:

Killer #1 – Who are you? No, really?

Most folks can smell a phony a mile away. Ladies, it's the
guys you start talking to at a party and he reeks of his own
mess. You know the one, talking loud, dressed loud, over
compensating because he's not really comfortable with his
own self.

In all seriousness, never be superficial. The average
relationship is founded on the sharing of similar likes or
opinions or building common ground. It is impossible to find
out these things or build a stronger bond with a person in
order to go deeper than just a friendly chit chat if you don't
first give off authenticity. You'll only find a dead end with
somebody if you're trying to build a relationship of trust, but
their intention is only to look out for #1 - themselves.

Killer #2 – Can I trust you?

To earn someone's trust, you must make it a point to show the person you're connecting with that they can trust you. One way of doing this is to remain open and receptive yourself.

You should never let people feel like they have to earn your trust in the beginning. If you remain guarded until people prove themselves trustworthy, you're going to be waiting a long time, my friend!

If your attitude projects, "I've tried to do things in the past and gotten hurt, so I'm not going to do anything for anybody" then don't worry about connecting. At that point everyone's trying to avoid you!

Your attitude should be welcoming and inviting. People gravitate towards positivity so avoid being a skeptic and instead a low your positive energy to draw people into you.

Killer #3 – Next in line, please!

Don't treat people like transactions. Meaning, don't treat people as if they only have one singular purpose and that your relationship with them is based strictly on "the deal". You've exchanged business cards and now it's only about the immediate sale. The relationship ends right there. "Alright, here's my card, I need you to do this for me." Ugh. Never treat people like transactions.

Killer #4 – Making Everything About Yourself

You should never be 'one-sided'. One-sidedness happens when you keep it cool with somebody just to get a job, a connection or access. In nightclubs, a lot of people will try to get cool with the club owners or people that work the door just in order to be able to get in or get free drinks.

You'll quickly find that being one-sided will leave you empty-handed when it comes to making connections.

Killer #5 – Making Asumptions

Experts say that over 95% of people form an opinion of people within the first 10 seconds. The problem with doing that is you tend to make assumptions about that individual and when you assume things before getting to know that person you become the first 3 letters of ASSumption.

Your asking for problems when you make assumptions. Don't be afraid to ask for clarification.

Let's talk about Social Networking no-no's!

Killer #6 – Social NOT working

If you're on a social networking or media site, whether it be Twitter, Facebook, or LinkedIn, don't send generic personal messages. This is the fastest way to get removed or un-followed.

I believe with social media 80 percent of your focus should be on letting people get to know you. The other 20 percent is your business. And that's *after* they've had conversations and you establish a common ground.

Let's say I'm on Twitter and I follow someone and immediately receive a generic message that says, "Thanks for following me! Go to www.wasteoftime.com and get your free secret of XYZ." I just remove them. It's a waste of my time and above that, it's impersonal. They've already showed me what my worth to them is.

However, if I put a good Tweet out and somebody responds with "Yes get in touch with me!" or something like that, then we can build a really good relationship because it's authentic. I know it means something. I know it's directly to me. And when you have thousands of fans, followers, or connections, you really start getting a lot of different requests and opportunities. My advice is to only pay attention to authentic responses.

Killer #7 – Liar, Liar

Nothing will kill a relationship more than making promises you cannot or do not keep!

Nothing irritates me more than when I finally connect with someone at an event or a place, and they say, "I have a great person for you to meet. I'll email you the information." I really feel like we've connected, but then they never follow

through. It's so irritating.

We have a great conversation, I feel like we've connected, but they never follow through. So the next time I see that person, I immediately remember he never did what he said he would do. And I can't connect them.

Connecting Aspirations

I often get asked if there's anyone I haven't met – anyone that ranks high on my *List of People I'd Love to Meet*.
Absolutely!

I would love to connect with Oprah! I love the fact that she's such a giver. She's done so much to change people's lives. I would LOVE to do what Oprah does from giving and starting schools in other countries to having shows about the biggest gift. Just experiencing the gift of giving on that level would be a blessing. After being on the air for over 20 years, she's really branded herself. Her giving, changing and tapping into people's lives, is truly awe-inspiring.

I don't want to just be a motivational or inspirational speaker. That's why I really focus on building my business, not just speaking, because I want to give, especially financially. I want to give money back to people. My goal this year is to raise 1 million dollars for non-profits and charities.

Oprah inspires me to want to give more. She is one person that I would want to connect with. But not just to connect with to be on her show. I'd like to connect with her in her life; to be a friend. To be somebody that she can mentor.

Nike's Secret of Success

I read so many books and blogs, and I've listened to so many speakers at events, on YouTube and podcast and none of them have ever given a secret to success that I feel Nike has given. It's not hidden in 300 pages of a book or in 30-45 minutes of a speech.

It's simply the three most exciting action words of all time! Let's all say it together, "JUST DO IT!!!"

When you think of all the greats that just seemed to stumble upon success, they all were doing what Nike tells us to do every day. Just do it. You don't have to know everything. As a matter of fact the more you don't know about it the better. They say ignorance on fire is better than knowledge on ice and I believe that wholeheartedly. If you want to do something different in life like a job, relationship or even a connection with somebody you really look up to just do it.

In "The Alchemist" by Paulo Chuello, he says when you're doing what you're supposed to be doing all the universe conspires in helping you to achieve it. One thing I have discovered in life is this: Most people who are really, really smart never get around to starting a business because they try to wait until every single thing is perfect. All the while a "Rich Idiot" as referenced by Robert Shemin in his book "Why is This Idiot Rich and I'm Not" comes along and just does it. And then, the smart person is mad that it's not as good or up to par as he thinks it should be!!!

Take the next 60 seconds and really tell yourself the next time you get an inspired thought that you will *take action* and at least get started on it.

Action Steps from Chapter 8:

- TAKE ACTION TODAY! Too many people "plan to plan" and never take the first step. How many times have you had an idea only to see it on TV or being used by someone else months later. Imagine if you'd taken the steps to put that plan into action immediately, how much farther along you'd be today!

- Put 10 business cards in your pocket tomorrow morning. Do not allow your head to hit the pillow tomorrow night until you've both given and received 10 business cards from people that you can help (and who can help you)!

Take Away Lessons from Chapter 8:

✓ Remember the 7 Connection Killers the next time you meet someone: Don't be superficial, Create trust, Don't treat people like transactions, Don't be one-sided, EXCHANGE business cards, No generic Twitter messages, Don't Lie!

✓ Don't forget the Bonus Relationship Builder – Keep Your Promises!

Make a list of the people you'd like to connect with and then develop a plan to actually meet them!

Connect & Grow *Rich*

<u>NOTES</u>

Chapter 9

The Power of Asking

"IT'S NOT WHAT YOU KNOW OR WHO YOU KNOW BUT WHO YOU WILL ASK."

- ROB COATS

Getting help from people is one of the main reasons for establishing a large network, but if you never take the time to tap into your network you will waste not only valuable time but valuable resources as well.

I've read that most people do things for 2 reasons in life: to avoid pain and/or to gain pleasure. For a lot of us, asking for help isn't an easy thing. Usually at a very early age we've asked for something and were either scolded for asking or hurt in some other way as a result, and that experience has shaped our current reality. Most people would rather suffer than actually take the chance and get help to fix the problem. I will do my best at helping you to overcome this hurdle in your life.

Most people don't like asking for help when networking because it makes them feel vulnerable. They feel that they will either become indebted to that person, sometimes for life, or that it makes them inferior to that person.

I recently read a blog post by Dr. Deb (a psychologist that specializes in trauma and depression) who was interviewed

for The Tyra Banks Show on How To Ask For Help This is
what she listed as being some of the most common myths that
hold people back from asking today:

The Power of Asking

Myth: Asking for help makes us look vulnerable.

Truth: Asking for help creates an atmosphere of
empowerment. It communicates to others that, while you may
not have the answers, you are willing to find them and make
things better.

Myth: Holding things in and keeping personal issues under
wraps keeps us secure.

Truth: The person who can speak the most freely about his/
her life's trials and tribulations, and about their personal
and professional desires, is often the person who is most
comfortable about themselves and their goals, and has
accepted their place in life. In reality, not allowing yourself
to be "known" keeps you socially isolated, and therefore,
insecure. When you seek the counsel of others, you'll not
only connect with them, but you'll also realize that you're not
alone in your struggle.

Myth: It may be a bother to others.

Truth: Doing it all can do you in. Being too self-sufficient

can create stress levels that tip your physical, emotional and spiritual scales.

Myth: Highly successful people never ask for help.

Truth: Actually, successful individuals will tell you that the key to success is knowing your strengths and weaknesses. Learning how to delegate, asking for help and letting others show you the way are part of the plan. Successful people are driven and motivated -- and when the going gets tough, the tough ask for help!

Myth: I am a giver. I don't like when others help me.

Truth: Get over it. With practice, you'll learn to be comfortable when others help you. And before long, you'll come to realize that you deserve a helping hand every now and then.

Remember:

- Have realistic expectations for the kind of help you are seeking

- Express your needs simply and clearly

- Let others know you are there to help them as well

- Praise your pals for their assistance and pat yourself in the back for asking for help

"If you know how to ask… you shall receive"

I know many of us are all too familiar with the statement of conventional wisdom: "Ask and you shall receive", but what if we could take it one step further and say: "If you know how to ask you shall receive." The better you know how to ask for help the better your chances will be of getting help. In the book **Smart Networking** by Liz Lynch, she states: "Asking for something that can easily be fulfilled creates positive feelings and strengthens the relationship. Asking for something outrageous that doesn't materialize can cause negative feelings on both sides." She continues to add that you can create an uncomfortable and unnecessary tension in the relationship when you put your contacts in a position of saying no to you. Often, when someone can't face telling you no, they may end up avoiding you altogether to escape the guilt and embarrassment. So "No" can actually hurt.

To increase the chances for success when you ask, you should really take the time to understand the situation from the other persons' point of view. When you're asking for help, the person is subconsciously, asking two questions: How easy is it to fulfill this request, and what's the value to me of fulfilling it?

In the 21st century it seems like everyone is focused on a "to do list", that needs to be done yesterday. So, when you ask

for something if you don't have a strong relationship with that person it should be something that they can do easily and quickly.

As far as the second phase of the question… what's the value to them? For some, the value to them is just being able to help you get one step further, but for others, they will look at it and ask themselves: "is this helping me to further my goals." If people know, like, and trust you they will generally be open to helping you.

However if the request is challenging you should look at how that person can get a tangible benefit. Try to present the request in terms that show the benefit to that person such as financial reward, or positive publicity, or perhaps even the possibility of future connection.

Asking helps you organize your thinking as well. Think through your questions before you go into a situation.

When it comes to asking for help it seems that there are only two types of people in the world: those who are too independent (feel like help will bruise their ego) or the completely co-dependent crowd (those who are too shy or feel awkward). It doesn't have to be this way.

Find a balance between these 2 extremes by remembering these key points:

- People in your support network like to help. They love you and want you to succeed.

- It's okay to make mistakes. No one expects you to be perfect. Allow yourself the chance to screw up royally - it's a great learning experience.

- You're stronger than you think. 51 percent of what you think you need help for can be done by you if you simply take action.

9 Factors Of Asking

1. What type of help you need- Be specific. Let people know exactly what it is you want so they can know how to assist you.

2. Why you need it – People will respond better if you can relate to them a larger purpose or give them a greater understanding of the reason for the task to be completed and sometimes even why they are the best one to fulfill the obligation.

3. When you need it – Don't be afraid to give a deadline or date for completion of the task. This will only further serve to reiterate the importance of the task at hand.

4. Know to ask for help before frustration and anger

take over. This is the first and most important step. If you're an "overdoer" and want to handle things by yourself, it may not be as easy to identify what exactly you'll need help with. Take a few minutes to ponder this.

5.   Leave behind feelings of shame and embarrassment. Just because you're asking for help doesn't mean you're a failure. It's actually wise and a very successful strategy because it will save stress and time.

6.   Talk to someone who you're close to-- like a friend or family member-- if you're feeling a bit intimidated asking for help from someone else. Maybe they can point you in the right direction. Think about what will happen if the situation is not dealt with and all the weight is on your shoulders.

7.   State clearly what it is that would be helpful and be specific. People generally want to help they just need to know exactly what is expected of them.

8.   Abstain from whining when you're doing too much; it will turn people away. Be positive and you'll have the support of people around who will often pitch in on their own if they feel you're

deserving of help because of the kind of person you are.

9. Say thank you. Always be grateful and appreciative when someone has done something to help. That way if you'll need to ask for help again they will be happy and willing to give a hand. Remember to help others too.

When you practice these simple truths you are much more likely to get help when asking than to not get it at all.

Hint: Don't let your pride be the reason that you don't get help. Help is inevitable when you ask in the right way.

Action Steps from Chapter 9:

- What are you struggling with right now? Copywriters exist to help people write better and sell more. Personal trainers exist to help people with weight loss. Business coaches exist to help people grow their business. Someone out there can help you with your current struggles. Reach out and ask them for help.

- Create a list of questions to guide you when asking for assistance. Questions detailing what you need, deadlines you're facing, and reminding you to ask what you can do for the other person as well.

Take Away Lessons from Chapter 9:

✓ Don't be afraid to ask for help.

✓ No one is immune from needing assistance. No one is too famous, too rich, or too successful to need help from someone at some point.

The Bible says, "Pride goeth before a fall." Don't let your pride get in the way of reaching out for assistance. Failing may be a great lesson to learn about, but if you don't have to fail – why do it?

Connect & Grow *Rich*

<u>NOTES</u>

Chapter 10

Using Social Media to Connect

"IF A MAN DOES NOT MAKE NEW ACQUAINTANCES AS HE ADVANCES THROUGH LIFE, HE WILL SOON FIND HIMSELF ALONE."

- SAMUEL JOHNSON

We are in the information age. Social networking sites are online communities in which users can find and interact with other users who share common interests. If you plan to connect in life you need to build a presence online. You cannot ignore the power of social networking, it is immediate and informative. Hundreds of millions of people are involved and the internet is still in its early stages!

People are pretty polarized about the social media craze. It's an Internet tug-of-war between the believers and the non-believers. And one by one, the believers (the users) are dragging the non-believers (the non-users) across the line. Which one are you?

Social media, or social networking, has taken the world by storm. Actually, by tsunami! It's a tidal wave of people, photos, videos and tweets that equal massive connections. The big six - Facebook, YouTube, LinkedIn, Twitter, Ning, and Flickr pretty much dominate the market. If you're going to play in the social media world, those five are the sandbox.

Everyone else that's not in the big six goes into their branding meetings wishing their name was LinkedIn.

If you are new to connecting all the social networking sites might be overwhelming. Should you prioritize? Yes.

Are You LinkedIn?

If you register with only one site it should be LinkedIn. It is literally an online resume. The structure of the site lends creditability to users as they make connections. One cannot just "accept" friendships on LinkedIn. There is an expectation of personal connection. To be added to someone's network you need know the person.

LinkedIn is a business network. It's social networking on a business level. I've gotten everything from opportunities to speak in different states and cities to consultation jobs for as much as $250,000 simply because I took the time to develop my profile on LinkedIn. It's not all about pictures either. You can upload videos too. It's an interactive business card saying to the world, "This is my business. This is what I do." The more questions you answer on different sites, the more you are perceived as an expert. It allows you to brand yourself in any way you want. Because it is a business-oriented social site, you will want to maintain a certain level of professionalism on LinkedIn. It can cost you dearly in networking if you're not careful.

Practical Application: - all business, all opportunity, all connections. But it's a giant leads club until someone figures out what their value proposition is, and how to deliver it. The key right now is to build a base of connections and consistently deliver value messages to attract more.

The Buzz on Twitter

I love Twitter because it allows you the ability to receive information. I get inspiration and daily education from the Internet and different blogs and posts. Just think; the more friends or followers one has, the more content and value they give. For example, look at Sean "P Diddy" Combs. He leaves a lot of inspirational messages and quotes for the day. He will talk about the fact that he's home, eating Cheerios with his kids, say that God is great or tweet that he's in the studio. His statuses and updates make you feel like you've spent your day with him without actually being there or really "knowing" him. You may go through a rough spell where you think, "Man I need some inspiration now." So you check his Twitter statuses and updates and other famous people to find that they are saying the same things.

You shoot them a message and they may respond to you. This presents an awesome opportunity to network with them.

Twitter also gives you the ability to send constant, up to the minute information about yourself or your company, as well as provides you with opportunities to meet like

minded professionals. This combination can lead to a high level of personal branding and can provide endless business opportunites.

Practical Application - newest of the social media, it's gibberish to some, money to others, and mystery to most. I tweet one value message every day. I tweet my own thoughts and words. And I recommend you do the same. Bottom line: Twitter is a great way to drive traffic to your main site.

Secret: If you want to be relevant on twitter,
tweet something relevant.
- Jeffrey Gitomer

Tip: Never underestimate the power of the "retweet"!

Facebook – Friends and Fans

Facebook is great for both networking and connecting. Facebook lets you see that the person you may want to connect with or that you may admire is, in fact, a real person. Take Bob Harper from NBC's The Biggest Loser. He is one of the most successful weight-loss coaches in the world. When you click on his profile, it's rarely about the TV show. You'll see him at a BBQ, you'll see him at his friend's house, you'll see him at a party, and you'll also see him behind the scenes on the show. Facebook turns Bob Harper the "TV guy" into "My Friend Bob" – the real person. Most of the time, the comments his friends leave on his page are a testament to the kind of person that he is. What LinkedIn is for business networking, Facebook is for social connecting.

Practical Application: So now you have found your old high school or college friends - or better, they found you. That's your "social" page. The business question is, "Do you have a fan page?" A fan page is the way to give value and attract new friends and customers.

REALITY BYTES: Facebook was just valued at 9.5 billion dollars. A couple of 24 year olds that have changed the Internet forever in less than six years.

YouTube Superstars

Soulja Boy, a popular teen rapper, built his brand off of YouTube. He's made over $7 million and has one of the most popular songs, "Superman". He's a very successful artist. He sells shoes, clothes and is a producer. He makes millions of dollars branding himself on the Internet. He was discovered on the Internet.

Rachel Young owns Big Cheese Marketing and is a well-known direct response copywriter in her field. She created a YouTube video for her business that's been seen over 200,000 times – without ever telling one single person about it! Talk about the power of going viral!

Practical Application - if it's a video world, why are you without your HD Flip? As you know from MTV, video killed the radio star. I have a dedicated YouTube channel that I post sales tips and random rants about attitude, trust, loyalty and other business value points. How are you taking advantage of YouTube? Where are your customer video testimonials when you really need them?

The sites we've discussed are a huge platform to connect with the people you want if you can get behind them. Too many business owners are resistant to change thinking that these sites are impersonal. You hear them asking, "Why is everybody on Twitter?" or "Why is everyone on their

Blackberry?" If you are flexible and willing to try something new to grow and connect, you will find incredible resources and people.

There are key words to consider as you try to build your social media world. Connections, attraction, video, value, consistency, fan, relevance, write, allocate, monetize. Keep these words in mind as you begin to develop your social presence and focus your personal brand.

And then there's YOU - The largest element in social media or social networking is you. What you do, what you post, what you tweet, what you shoot, what you record, and the work (dedication) to make your personal message and your personal brand attractive. But there's a secret. How you position and promote yourself in the NON-social media world is critical to your success in the social media world. Your writing, your website, your blog, your ezine, your personal brand in your marketplace, your perceived value in the marketplace, and your reputation, are elements of attraction that affect your social media status - and surely your success.

And then there are the charlatans and those trying to take unfair advantage of others. Like anything else in business there will always be a small percentage of idiots and zealots doing the wrong thing - ignore them, don't let the actions of a few spoil your outlook to advance and grow.

Social media provides excellent examples of how relationships can bloom and grow on the Net. You can reconnect to countless friends from college and high school. You can see what is going on with them via status updates and notes (often imported blog posts). You can converse quickly through wall posts, chat and direct messages. You can check your network on most mobile devices and interact from wherever you may be. You can network through different networks via Facebook and LinkedIn through group message boards and get invites to upcoming events. While there are some drawbacks to social media, truthfully, it has changed the way we socialize with many friends, new and old.

While technology can bring people closer together, social networks are still only the first level where you can generally foster initial connections. Connections need to be cemented through other means of communication to become more meaningful.

Also, in addition to your social media sites, remember these connecting tools:

Blog- If you build a network of people where they continue to come to read your thoughts, companies will pay you big money for advertising.

Ezine - (electronic magazine) or a newsletter lets you stay in

touch and overtime by continuing to give value when you put a product out they will buy it from you just because you've added so much value.

Use social media to let you start building your brand. You can become as big as you want or you can keep a relatively low profile. Invest time, effort, and commitment and it will take you anywhere you want to go.

Action Steps from Chapter 10:

- When requesting friends on any social networking site, keep in mind that you're growing your business at the same time. Make sure your new "friends" aren't leaving explicit comments on your profile which could potentially turn off any business ventures which may come in the future.

- Did you read an article that one of your connections may find useful? See a book that someone may be interested in? Don't hesitate to send your connections content that they can use! You're solidifying connections by taking the focus off of yourself!

Take Away Lessons from Chapter 10:

✓ When you're resistant to change, the world will pass you by.

✓ Know which sites are for business networking or connecting and maintain that level of professionalism.

Don't be afraid to reach out to those you think are unreachable because of their celebrity status. You never know who'll respond and that could lead to something even greater!

<u>NOTES</u>

Chapter 11

Transforming Your Connections by Being Remarkable

"TAKE THE FIRST STEP IN
FAITH. YOU DON'T HAVE TO
SEE THE WHOLE STAIRCASE,
JUST TAKE THE FIRST STEP."

- DR. MARTIN LUTHER KING JR.

Writing this book has connected me to you, the reader. I want to share my experience because I know everyone can live and leave a legacy. I hope this book has inspired you to move past your fears and taught you the power of connection vs the inaction of networking. Here are some final points.

Be an Excellent Receiver

T. Harv Eker says, "You have to be an excellent giver and an excellent receiver."

Most of the time, wealthy people are more open to receive and poor people aren't.

So many people feel they deserve to make a certain amount of money. They feel that if someone gives to them, it's taking away from someone else. That's not true! When you deliver **TRUE** value to another individual, they are being richly rewarded for your knowledge and expertise.

T. Harv Eker has an example where he asks, "Which one

of your arms is more important, your left arm or your right arm?" The answer, he says, "is both. Both arms are equally important." Just like giving is important, receiving is important. So be good at adding value first and then when it's time for someone to bless you, receive it. There's nothing wrong with receiving... from the right person.

Here's an example to show you that not all gifts will be worth receiving!

In the countryside of India the Buddha is giving a talk on Dharma. Whenever the Buddha speaks, people gather from all around to listen to his wisdom. On this particular occasion there is a heckler in the crowd. As Buddha talks the heckler is always interrupting, trying to get a rise of anger from Buddha. Over time the man become more and more abusive. Finally after a long period the Buddha addresses the heckler. "Sir", the Buddha asks, "may I ask a question of you?" The heckler laughs and replies, "Yes I would be happy to give you my wisdom". The Buddha then says, "Sir if you have a gift to give a friend, but the friend refuses to accept the gift, who then does the gift belong?" The man thinks for a moment and states, "Well I guess the gift belongs to me." The Buddha smiles and looks at the man and says "Well sir, thank you but I cannot accept your gift of abuse."

You will always have people who want to belittle your

dreams. Mark Twain said, "Keep away from people who try to belittle your ambitions. Small people always do that, but the really great make you feel that you, too, can become great."

In that regard, it's ok to refuse the dream-stealers and idea-crushers who would take away your dreams of success.

Magna Cum Laude
of the School of Hard Knocks

People will question you. They want to know whether you have a Ph.D. or what qualifies you to do what you do.

When I first started connecting to create wealth, I hadn't finished school, but I majored in the School of Hard Work, earned a Master's in Entrepreneurship and received my Ph.D. in succeeding in the Business of Life.

Add Value First

"If you wish to climb higher, then lift others up."
–Ralph Marston

Today and every day, deliver more than you are getting paid to do. The victory of success will be yours when you learn the secret of putting out more than is expected in all you do.

I studied the top five internet marketers online (the ones that make millions of dollars in 24 hours etc) and the one thing they all did consistently is give tons of information out before they asked you for your credit card information. In their blogs or YouTube videos it seems as if they give out their most valuable information. In the eyes of the consumer, when they see how much they have already received for free, the perception becomes that the information they don't have will be even more worth investing in.

While information is so accessible now because of the internet the thing that will make you stick out compared to your competition is what you give and this reflects in the quality of the product or service that you give. Give your best stuff first and get a loyal list of friends. Remember friends are the ones you don't need to sell because they've already bought into you.

The Power of Gifts- They go further than you ever could have imagined. Think about this: When someone is going to meet a King, in order to get in good graces, they give a gift. When you find favor in the eyes of the king, you can expect great things to come.

"Give every man more in use value than you take from him in use value, than you take from him in cash value; then you are adding to the life of the world with every business transaction"
– Wallace D. Wattles

Mike Murdoch said, "One day of favors is worth a thousand days of labor."

You only need one person and one opportunity. With an encounter at Max and Erma's I solved a problem for two people, and I was able to reap hundreds of thousands of dollars as a result.

All you need is one person to believe in your dreams, your ideas and in what you're doing. That's the difference between the season of lack and the season of advantage.

In her book *People Power*, Donna Fisher refers to the boomerang effect. According to Fisher, "Taking the initiative to give, participate and offer support to your network is similar to throwing a boomerang. Eventually what you inject into your network, opportunities, information, support and energy, and additional contacts comes back to you."

Connect With The End In Mind

I've learned that people will forget what you said, people will forget what you did, but people will never forget how you made them feel.

This is one of the most important principles in this book.

I met a guy at a networking event a couple months back who

was a big anchor/analyst for the most watched sports network. (ESPN) We were having a great conversation when I asked him what was one the experiences that pushed him to getting to the level he was at now. He told me that several years back he was at an event like the one we were at and he tried to approach a guy to get some advice on how he could also get to that level. The guy was a professional athlete now turned analyst that had experienced a fair amount of success in the industry. The answer he got is something he told me he would never forget. He said the guy was very short, looked down on him and when he went to shake his hand the guy never moved an inch. He said the guy told him he's not looking to lose his spot and that he should look for a new career because he wouldn't fit in.

After that conversation he promised not only would he take his job but he would never treat any one the way he had been treated. Years later he ended up getting a job at that station and became an even more respected analyst then the rude gentleman he had met previously. The guy who made that comment to him also doesn't work there anymore.

Treat Caterpillars Like Butterflies

No matter where someone is in life you should be careful to never judge them by their current situation. That's temporary thinking. 5 years from now you don't know where that person

will be and better yet how that connection can benefit you. This takes patience but a wise man makes more friends then enemies. Understand the things you do today will either bring you pain or pleasure in the near future.

How do millionaires and billionaires spend their free time? Playing golf. Why do you need to play golf? The most

---

"I will waste not even a precious second today in anger of hate or jealousy or selfishness. I know that the seeds I sow, I will harvest, because every action, good or bad, is always followed by an equal reaction. I will plant only good seeds this day."

– Og Mandino

Yes. You Need To Play Golf.

important reason needs to be the first sentence in the chapter. If that doesn't sell you on it here are a few others:

- Golf is the number one sport to connect with people.

- As much as 80% of business deals are done on the

golf course. Not the boardroom. While you are waiting with your awesome PowerPoint presentation the CEO took your colleague on a golf trip to Scotland. Think about it.

- When you get on the golf course, you can't have a cell phone. You can play two or three hours and spend that time with a person really studying them and seeing how they play and work.

- Success is about sacrifice. If it were easy it would be called sleeping. Learn to get comfortable with things that make you uncomfortable.

You can foster some dynamic relationships on the golf course.

Diamond Deals in Basketball Stands

Most public schools did not have middle school golf teams, my mentor wanted me to attend a preparatory school in upper Arlington, which is an elite suburb in the Columbus area, that would grant me the opportunity to play.

When I arrived, I was a little overwhelmed. These were some of the wealthiest families in the city, with their expensive luxury cars, million-dollar homes; even private jets.

This can be a little much for a 12-year old boy!

After my initial shyness, I began to establish relationships with my classmates, and even started to learn from their parents!

While playing basketball during my high school years, I would sit in the stands during the JV games to prepare mentally for my game that would take place next. I began to learn that parents would sometimes use this as an opportunity to network or connect.

One of the parents wanted a diamond for his wife, and another parent was in the diamond industry. I saw firsthand the deal that took place in the stands of a basketball game.

I realized this school and the other elite schools in the country did not necessarily have the best education, but rather the

connecting and the connection tools that can be utilized during and after school. From the best high school academies, to the top universities in the nation, you were paying for *connections*, not what you learned in the classroom.

So ultimately, one reason why connecting and building relationships is so important is because through connections there is never a problem you can't solve.

The person you want (perhaps NEED) to connect with most is just one or two people away. All you need are the tools described in this book and the guts to take the first step.

And the bigger problem you do solve will determine the pay off that you get. So it pays to help people with big problems. Yes, that's just the power of connections.

And it only happens when you start doing what you were put here to do.

My mother battled breast cancer.
My father lost his job.
I went through a period of financial depression.
I temporarily lived with my parents as an adult.
My parents lost their house in foreclosure.

But I came out of each struggle stronger, more confident, and a better person for having braved each situation and creating something from it.

I thoroughly believe and will tell anybody from any background that's ever went through anything in life, and been discouraged and been down, if I can do all these things and hold it together while all these things go on, so can you.

You've been armed with all the tools you need. Your connection to success is waiting. All you need to do is take the first step!

Action Steps from Chapter 11:

-   Always be prepared! If you sell a product, always carry one on you (or in your vehicle or briefcase). If you offer a service, never have a shortage of business cards. Remember my friend's mantra: Prosperity favors the prepared!

-   The world is your office. Never worry about surroundings when a deal presents itself. Make sure you've got pen and paper, your cell phone, or whatever you need to facilitate the process and just let it happen!

-   Don't wait. The person you've been waiting to connect with is only one or two people away! The time to take action is now. Find a way to connect with one person today!

Take Away Lessons from Chapter 11:

✓   Be an excellent receiver.

✓   Look for exceptions rather than rules.

✓   Take up the game of golf.

Do what you were put on earth to do and the world will truly beat a path to your door!

Connect & Grow *Rich*

<u>NOTES</u>

Chapter 12

*Closing Thoughts:
Take Away Lessons
& Action Steps*

Sometimes it's helpful to have everything at your fingertips, to help jumpstart your ideas and turn them into action.

Here I've put together all the Action Steps and Take Away Lessons for you to use as a "to do" list to maximize your success and business growth!

Chapter 1:

Action Steps

- Write down 3 ways you can take control of your current situation to make it better.

- Who do you know? Write down all of the people you currently know (regardless of whether they're in your industry or niche). Now write down the people you most WANT to know. Ask the people you know if they have contacts who could connect you with the people you WANT to know.

Take Away Lessons

✓ Connecting is about cultivating and nurturing relationships. You **both** must benefit from the arrangement!

✓ Most folks are tuned into WIIFM and want to see what kind of value you're bringing to the relationship – don't disappoint!

✓ Remember, it's not always about you! Make sure when you're connecting with someone that you bring value to the table!

✓ Don't try to sell someone too early. Make the connection on a deeper level than just swapping dollars for a product or service.

Chapter 2:

Action Steps

- Take a minute to look at yourself in the mirror right now. Is that the face, clothing, and attitude of a world class business owner? What actions do you need to take right now to change that?

- What *would* you do if you knew you couldn't fail? Take a few minutes to ponder that thought with closed

eyes. Then write your response down on paper. Now turn that idea into your own action steps and create the success you've always wanted!

Take Away Lessons

- ✓ If you can't believe in yourself, no one else will. Really concentrate on building and growing something you're proud to put your name on!

- ✓ Don't allow the lies of small-thinkers to belittle your dreams. If the success you desire was impossible, no one would ever have achieved it before! Bill Gates has billions of dollars! Warren Buffet has created an empire from being the lowest paid CEO in the world. Your dreams and successes are a direct result of what YOU want them to be!

- ✓ You become what you think about most. Concentrate on success!

Chapter 3:

Action Steps

- Your dream is dead in the water without a plan. Sit down right now and create 3 Action Steps you can

take immediately to start working on your own goals in life. Be specific!

- There were two very important reasons we were able to get Ryan the money he needed. First, was the use of social networking websites. Facebook allows you to have a maximum of 5,000 members. Have you maxed out your friends yet? Request new friends daily to maximize the number of eyes that see what you're offering!

- The second important reason we were successful was the use of friends and family. The one's you hold dearest want to see you succeed. Don't hesitate to ask for help and advice from your elders or other family members who have been successful!

Take Away Lessons

- ✓ Don't be afraid to add value. Above and beyond what you think the other person is expecting.

- ✓ Sometimes your biggest helpers come from the most unlikeliest of places!

Chapter 4:

Action Steps

Power Connector:

1. Stay connected: Write an email, send a text or call at least once every two weeks to remain fresh in their minds and continue to build the know, like and trust.

2. Solve Problems: Find out what their biggest need is and start working to help them fill it. This will make you much more valuable than the person who is just calling to take them to lunch and pick their brain.

3. Make it Personal: There is nothing more powerful than sending a meaningful note that expresses your appreciation for everything someone has done. Send a card or personal gift in the mail. Make it personable and they will make it pleasurable.

Potential Connectionaire:

1. Stay connected: Endeavor to stay connected with the weak ties with emails or newsletters. You never know if they have a consulting gig or business opportunity that is perfect for you.

2. Reply to E-mail: No matter how many e-mails you receive each day, you can still reply to your weak ties with brief responses. If you are pressed for time then keep it to one sentence or write to tell them you will respond later.

3. Be strategic but thoughtful: **Strategic you**: Go through your network and pick out two or three connections that you may not know that well but would like to know better. **Thoughtful you:** Pick out an article online or send them a friendly note. This will show tem that you take the time to think about them and are open to building a stronger connection.

Take Away Lessons

✓ When you're resistant to change, the world will pass you by. Don't make the same mistake MySpace made!

✓ Know which sites are for business networking or connecting and maintain that level of professionalism.

✓ Don't be afraid to reach out to those you think are unreachable because of their celebrity status. You never know who'll respond and could lead to something much greater!

✓ Remember the key steps to get started: Know Your Surroundings, Start Reading, Prepare Your Introduction, and Just Do It!

✓ Get a mentor like the Connectionaire™ to take years off your learning curve and ease your transition into successful connector!

✓ Don't forget your tools! Get business cards, make

your presence known online, get people talking about yourself!

✓ Take advantage of free social networking sites to start connecting immediately!

Chapter 5:

Action Steps

- Set aside at least 15 minutes a day to study the body language of other people, as well as acquiring a conscious awareness of your own gestures. A good reading ground is anywhere that people meet and interact. Social functions, business meetings, parties, airports or church are good places to observe the entire spectrum of human gestures.

Take Away Lessons

✓ Recognize that people communicate on many levels. Watch their facial expressions, eye contact, posture, hand and feet movements, body movement and placement, and appearance and passage as they walk toward you. Every gesture is communicating something if you listen with your eyes. Become accustomed to watching nonverbal communication and your ability to read nonverbal communication will

grow with practice.

✓   If a person's words say one thing and their body
     language says another, listen to the nonverbal
     communication –that is usually the correct decision.

Chapter 6:

Action Steps

-    Are you already connected with someone on a
     social networking site that could help you grow
     your business? Many celebrities, authors, and sports
     stars have profiles online that allow you to become
     "friends" with them. Using your list of people you
     WANT to be connected with from Chapter 1, find
     these stars on Twitter, Facebook, or LinkedIn and start
     connecting with them. Remember WIIFM! Establish
     a relationship first, then you can move on to business
     growth.

-    You'll notice the connection success stories in this
     chapter outweigh the horror stories. Don't be afraid
     to make a connectionship with someone who could
     benefit you. Rachel Young says, "Prosperity favors the
     prepared." Don't wait until tomorrow to start making
     your connections online! The web is open 24/7!

Take Away Lessons

✓ Your success as a connector depends on giving value first and planting profitable seeds.

✓ You never know how close you are to meeting the person you most want to see until you ask the people you know.

✓ Don't ever quit. You could be just one step away from the biggest success of your life!

✓ Establish the relationship first. Period.

✓ Remember the Dalai Lama's words, "When you lose, don't lose the lesson."

Chapter 7:

Action Steps

- Flip the script and find one person that YOU can give Private Information, Access to Diverse Skill Sets, and Power to. Remember, connectionships are a two-way street!

- If you haven't already, create profiles on LinkedIn, Facebook, and other social networking sites so you

can begin your online connectionships!

Take Away Lessons

✓ There are three main advantages to networking and connecting: Private Information, Access to Diverse Skill Sets, and Power.

✓ Private Information can mean you getting access to valuable material before your competition (but its relative, so be careful!)

✓ You honestly never know who you know that knows someone powerful! Accessing Diverse Skill Sets through your connections can take you farther than you ever thought possible!

✓ You don't have to have a business in order to start making connections. Keep in mind the Chinese Proverb, "Dig the well before you are thirsty"!

Chapter 8:

Action Steps

- TAKE ACTION TODAY! Too many people "plan to plan" and never take the first step. How many times have you had an idea only to see it on TV or being used by someone else months later. Imagine

if you'd taken the steps to put that plan into action immediately, how much farther along you'd be today!

- Put 10 business cards in your pocket tomorrow morning. Do not allow your head to hit the pillow tomorrow night until you've both given and received 10 business cards from people that you can help (and who can help you)!

Take Away Lessons

✓ Keep in mind the 7 Connection Killers the next time you meet someone: Don't be superficial, Create trust, Don't treat people like transactions, Don't be 'one-sided, EXCHANGE business cards, No generic Twitter messages, Don't Lie!

✓ Don't forget the Bonus Relationship Builder – Keep Your Promises!

✓ Make a list of the people you'd like to connect with and then develop a plan to actually meet them!

Chapter 9:

Action Steps

- What are you struggling with right now? Copywriters exist to help people write better and sell more.

Personal trainers exist to help people with weight loss. Business coaches exist to help people grow their business. Someone out there can help you with your current struggles. Reach out and ask them for help.

- Create a list of questions to guide you when asking for assistance. Questions detailing what you need, deadlines you're facing, and reminding you to ask what you can do for the other person as well.

Take Away Lessons

✓ Don't be afraid to ask for help.

✓ No one is immune from needing assistance. No one is too famous, too rich, or too successful to need help from someone at some point.

The Bible says, "Pride goeth before a fall." Don't let your pride get in the way of reaching out for assistance. Failing may be a great lesson to learn about, but if you don't have to fail – why do it?

Chapter 10:

Action Steps

- When requesting friends on any social networking site, keep in mind that you're growing your business

at the same time. Make sure your new "friends" aren't leaving explicit comments on your profile which could potentially turn off any business ventures which may come in the future.

- Did you read an article that one of your connections may find useful? See a book that someone may be interested in? Don't hesitate to send your connections content that they can use! You're solidifying connections by taking the focus off of yourself!

Take Away Lessons

✓ Listen. Some of the worlds' best opportunities come to those who keep their mouth shut.

✓ Don't be afraid of people who belittle you. Remember what Tony Robbins says, "People hate you when you succeed and love you when you fail."

Find favor with the right person and you'll go far.

Chapter 11:

Action Steps

- Always be prepared! If you sell a product, always carry one on you (or in your vehicle or briefcase). If

you offer a service, never have a shortage of business cards. Remember my friend's mantra: Prosperity favors the prepared!

- The world is your office. Never worry about surroundings when a deal presents itself. Make sure you've got pen and paper, your cell phone, or whatever you need to facilitate the process and just let it happen!

- Don't wait. The person you've been waiting to connect with is only one or two people away! The time to take action is now. Find a way to connect with one person today!

Take Away Lessons

✓ Be an excellent receiver.

✓ Look for exceptions rather than rules.

✓ Take up the game of golf.

Do what you were put on earth to do and the world will truly beat a path to your door!

I WILL ACT NOW. I WILL ACT NOW.
I WILL ACT NOW. HENCEFORTH, I
WILL REPEAT THESE WORDS EACH
HOUR, EACH DAY, EVERYDAY,UNTIL
THE WORDS BECOME AS MUCH A
HABIT AS MY BREATHING, AND THE
ACTION WHICH FOLLOWS BECOMES
AS INSTINCTIVE AS THE BLINKING
OF MY EYELIDS. WITH THESE WORDS
I CAN CONDITION MY MIND TO
PERFORM EVERY ACTION NECESSARY
FOR MY SUCCESS. I WILL ACT NOW. I
WILL REPEAT THESE WORDS AGAIN
AND AGAIN AND AGAIN. I WILL WALK
WHERE FAILURES FEAR TO WALK. I
WILL WORK WHEN FAILURES SEEK
REST. I WILL ACT NOW FOR NOW IS
ALL I HAVE. TOMORROW IS THE DAY
RESERVED FOR THE LABOR OF THE
LAZY. I AM NOT LAZY. TOMORROW IS
THE DAY WHEN THE FAILURE WILL
SUCCEED. I AM NOT A FAILURE. I
WILL ACT NOW. SUCCESS WILL NOT
WAIT. IF I DELAY, SUCCESS WILL
BECOME WED TO ANOTHER AND LOST
TO ME FOREVER. THIS IS THE TIME.
THIS IS THE PLACE. I AM THE PERSON.

- OG MANDINO

About the Author

GOOGLE ME 614-304-1017 cell
Connect with Rob @

Facebook www.facebook.com/addvaluefirst

Twitter: www.twitter.com/RobCoats

Linkedin: www.linkedin.com/in/robtcoats

Youtube: www.youtube.com/connectionaire

Rob periodically hosts Connect Your Life events and workshops in Ohio, NY and Atlanta, and you can find details about attending one (or having one at your office) at robcoats.com

You can reach him by email at robtcoats@gmail.com he does do consulting, and he reads all his mail.

For information on products, programs, and speaking availability, visit www.connectionaire.com